ROUGH NOTES

ON THE

STATE OF NEPAL

ROUGH NOTES

ON THE

STATE OF NEPAL

ITS GOVERNMENT, ARMY, AND RESOURCES

ORFEUR CAVANAGH

GYAN

Published by

GYAN

Gyan Publishing House
5, Ansari Road
Daryaganj, New Delhi-110002
Phone: 011-47034999, 9811692060
E-mail: books@gyanbooks.com

Distribution Network
gyanbooks.com
India, USA, Canada, UK, Australia

ISBN: 978-93-7133-335-1 (PB)

First Published, 1851

2nd Impression 2025

Printed at: Gyan Press, Delhi.

ROUGH NOTES ON THE STATE OF NEPAL
Author: ORFEUR CAVANAGH

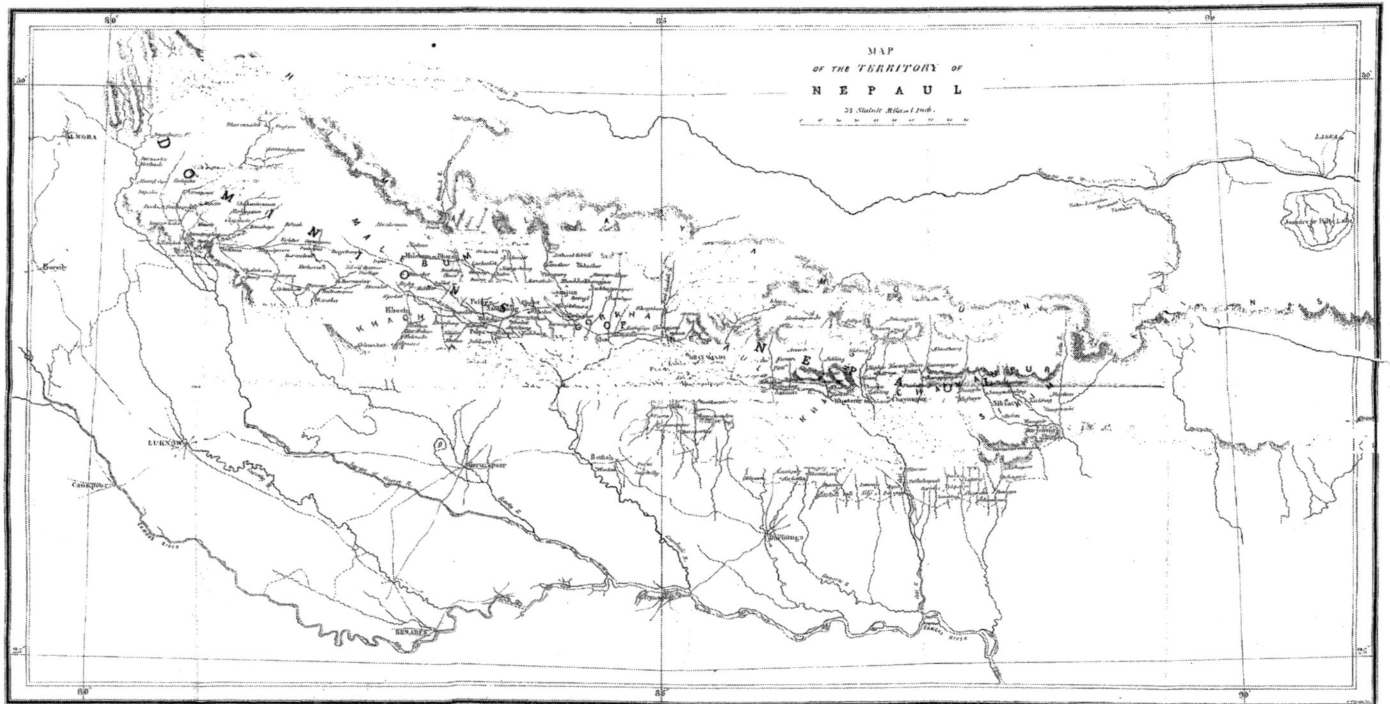
MAP
OF THE TERRITORY OF
NEPAUL
ALMORA
LUKNOW
BENARES
GORKHA
LASSA
GANGES RIVER

ROUGH NOTES

ON THE

STATE OF NEPAL,

ITS GOVERNMENT, ARMY, AND RESOURCES.

BY

CAPTAIN ORFEUR CAVENAGH,

32nd Regt. Bengal Native Infantry,

LATE IN POLITICAL CHARGE OF A MISSION FROM THE COURT AT KATHMANDHOO
TO HER MOST GRACIOUS MAJESTY.

Calcutta:

W. PALMER, MILITARY ORPHAN PRESS.

1851.

PREFACE.

From the date of my appointment to the Political charge of the Nepal Mission, I deemed it my duty to seize every opportunity of acquiring, in the course of my daily conversations with the Ambassador and his Sirdars, knowledge on every subject of interest connected with a country which has hitherto proved to Europeans almost a *terra incognita*, and regarding the Government and resources of which our information is still apparently so partial. I was subsequently fortunate enough to enjoy the advantage of being able to test by personal observation the value of the communications thus received, and I am bound in justice to acknowledge that, making due allowance for national vanity which naturally prompted a slight exaggeration, the statements put forth have proved extremely accurate. As a soldier my enquiries were principally directed towards the organization and discipline of the Nepal Army, a Force with which we may at any time be brought into collision, owing to, either the actual hostility of the Members of the Durbar, or their desire to rescue themselves from the thraldom of an insolent soldiery, even at the hazard of sacrificing the independence of their country. During the administration of the present Prime Minister, I am firmly convinced neither of these contingencies are likely to occur, for he is fully sensible of the great importance of our alliance and at the same time possesses far too much political sagacity and determination of character, ever to allow himself to become the puppet, even although he may strive to remain the favorite of the Army; but at a court where it may be said that for years past conspiracies have been of almost hourly, and assassinations of daily occurrence, it were vain to frame calculations based on the life of a single individual, and in the event of the death of General Jung Bahadur, not only is it reasonable to suppose that the bonds of discipline, as at present imposed upon the Gorkha troops, would become materially relaxed, and consequently the soldiery, like our late formidable opponents the Seikhs, degenerate into Prætorian bands, dictators alike dangerous to the stability of the Government they serve and to the repose of neighbouring States, but it is also not improbable that some of the Chiefs of the Pandee faction might succeed to power, and as the Members of this party have, I believe, invariably been opposed to the introduction of liberal measures and the spread of enlightened ideas, it may be inferred that they are imbued with all the prejudices of bigoted Hindus and doubtless inimical to the British power in India.

CHAPTER I.

Military Force of Nepal—Numerical strength—Nominal roll of Regiments—Commissioned and Non-Commissioned Officers—Commander-in-Chief and Staff—Rates of pay of different ranks—Jagirs—Commissions—Punjunnie, or annual re-enrolment—Leave—Description of Gorkha Soldiers—Discipline—Drill—Artillery—Ammunition, Arms and Accoutrements—Uniform—Want of Commissariat and Camp Equipage—General observations regarding the probable result of a war with the British, including an account of the different passes leading from the Plains to the Valley of Kathmandhoo, &c. &c.

In accordance with data which I have been enabled to collect from various sources, I am induced to estimate the strength of the Gorkha Army as at the utmost 25, or 26,000 men, of which nearly two-thirds are attached to the Regular Battalions and the remainder composed of Local or Irregular Corps. It is extremely difficult to ascertain with any degree of certainty the exact number of Regiments, as, unlike those attached to the Armies of European States, they bear no numbers, but are designated either by the names of Hindoo Divinities, or according to some peculiar quality with which the Soldiers of any particular Battalion have the reputation of being endowed; and perhaps, occasionally, as is the case with several of the corps of the Bengal Army, after some distinguished Officer by whom they may have been either raised or commanded. The following is a list of those Regiments with whose names I have become acquainted either from having personally witnessed them on Parade or heard them alluded to by members of the Mission.

Ram Dul,	Artillery.
Gunnès Dul,	ditto.
Rifle Regiment,	Infantry.

Latter,	Infantry.
Sri Nath,	"
Raj Dul,	"
Mor Indra Dul,	"
Sher Dul,	"
Kali Prasad (formerly Hanuman) Dul,	"
Ram Prithi Dul,	"
Debi Dul,	"
Jagat Dul,	"
Gorakh Nath,	"
Kali Baksh,	"
Sir bá doz,	"
Ba'zabani,	"
Ram Prya Dul,	"
Singhi Nath,	"
Naya Gorakh Nath,	"
Subz Dul,	"
Bhairav Nath,	"
Shumsher Dul,	"
Sri Mer,	"
Ran Sen,	"
Shah Baz,	"

Ballam Jung,	Infantry.
Suldar Jung,	"
Tara Nath,	"
Baithak Dul,	"
Chandi Baksh,	"
Sri Dut,	"
Gaur Baksh,	"
Chammud Nath,	"
Sri Daman,	"
Samna Jung,	"

A large force, consisting of 16 Regular and 1 Irregular Regiment, is stationed at the capital, Kathmandhoo, and in its immediate vicinity, and, as far as I can judge, the remaining corps are distributed amongst the different posts and fortresses on the British and Thibet frontiers, as detailed below :

Palpa, - - - -	2	Regular,	2	Irregular.
Peutana, - - - .	1	"		"
Saliana, - - - -	1	"		"
Sil Gurhee, - - -	2	"		"
Jamba (Thibet), -	2	"		"
Opudheea Gurhee,	"	"	1	"

Seesa Gurhee, -	,,	Regular,	1	Irregular.
Mukwanpore, - -	1	,,		,,
Hurripore, - - -	,,	,,	1	,,
Sinda Gurhee, - -	1	,,		,,
Dhankoota, - - -	1	,,		,,
Chowdanda, - -		,,	1	,,
Khutta Bunga (Terai)	2	,,		,,

The strength of Regiments, more especially of those employed on Police Duties which are, in some instances, 1,000 strong, varies, but the average of that of corps of the line may be fairly calculated at 600 Sepoys; with the exception of one or two Regiments, the complement of Commissioned and Non-Commissioned officers is on an extremely limited scale, not consisting of more than 1 Captain, 1 Lieutenant, 1 Subahdar, 6 Jemadars, 6 Havildars and 6 Naiks to a Battalion of 6 Companies.

The Commander-in-Chief is assisted by a Staff of 9 or 10 General Officers and Colonels, each of whom commands two or three Regiments, a Major (styled Burra Captain) and a Burra Adjutant or Adjutant General, whose duties appear in a great measure confined to the issue in a loud tone of the words of command on the occasion of a grand review. The emoluments appertaining to the command of the Army, derived principally from the annual gifts presented by the Sirdars and Soldiery, amount to about a Lac of Rupees per annum; the pay of officers of the higher ranks is not apparently regulated by any fixed standard but depends entirely on the favor or caprice of the Prime Minister, the rates of that granted to those of the lower grades, to Non-Commissioned Officers and Soldiers, are according to the following scale:

	Nepal Rupees per Annum.
Captains,	3,000 to 4,000
Lieutenants,	1,500 to 3,000
Subahdars,	1,000 to 1,500
Jemadars,	400 to 1,000
Havildars and Naiks,	200 to 600
Sepoys,	100 to 300

In addition to which all ranks are furnished every 7th or 8th year with a suit of uniform and also receive from the State the distinctive ornaments worn in the turban. It must, however, be understood that of the sums noted above only a very small proportion is actually paid from the Public Treasury, the remainder being realized from the profits derived from Jagirs or grants of Land conferred by the Government upon Officers and Soldiers, which profits must naturally fluctuate according to the seasons and also to the degree of labor and attention bestowed upon the soil. I believe that General Jung Bahadur is desirous of changing the present arrangement and would prefer adopting the system obtaining in European Armies of paying the troops at certain fixed rates according to rank, but the idea is repugnant to the feelings of the Sirdars, and should he attempt to introduce it against their inclination, he may run some little risk of sapping his present influence and power.

Officers receive duly signed commissions from the Rajah and are thereby empowered to administer justice and to award fines, not to exceed 100 rupees, amongst the peasantry residing on the Jagirs assigned for their support; as the fines thus levied are a perquisite of office, this privilege is doubtless occasionally abused.

Every male throughout the territory of Nepal is liable to be called upon to serve as a Soldier for one year, at the expiration of which period he is entitled to claim his discharge, but the power thus possessed by the Government of summoning recruits to its standards is, I should imagine, hardly ever exercised, for by all accounts there is no want of candidates for Military Service, on the contrary there are numerous applicants for employment, and at the general re-enrolment styled Punjunnie, which takes place annually during the Dusserah, when the ranks are not only weeded of weakly and inefficient Officers and Men, but the opportunity also taken of removing those to whom the Minister in power may prove unfavorable, the greatest interest is generally made by persons of all grades to prevent being remanded to their homes; corps on out-post duty, which owing to their distance from the Capital may not be subject to inspection at the Punjunnie, are usually disbanded on their return from command, new Regiments being raised in their stead, and the Officers and Soldiers composing them proceeding to their native villages, where they reside until fortunate enough to re-obtain service; thus a very large proportion of the population are instructed in the use of arms, and the army could, in a few months, be raised with little difficulty to 50,000 men. The system of re-enrolment applies equally to Civil as to Military Officers. Public functionaries out of employ are styled Daereeahs and distinguished by wearing white clothing.

Leave is generally granted to a portion of the troops between the months of March and June to enable them to assist in the cultivation of their lands, but the number to whom the indulgence is allowed does not appear to be defined, but to be entirely dependent on the will of the Minister, without whose sanction no man can be absent from his duty more than a month, little authority being vested in the hands of Colonels of Regiments, although no officer can obtain that rank who is not a relative of the Premier.

With the exception of the Newar tribe, who are considered deficient in courage, men of all castes are admitted into the Nepal Army and hitherto associated in the same Regiments without reference to religious prejudices; but General Jung Bahadur, having apparently studied the doctrines laid down by European Politicians on the subject of the balance of power, has recently introduced the system of forming distinct corps of Rajputs, Muggurs, Gurungs and Krats, thus, as any class feeling or jealousy which may exist amongst these different tribes, although perhaps not fostered, is certainly not discouraged by the Government, in the event of a mutiny breaking out in any one Regiment, there would be little dread of the spirit of disaffection becoming general, and in all probability it could be easily subdued; moreover a greater spirit of emulation and *esprit de corps* is thereby engendered amongst the Soldiers than under the old regulation of attaching them indiscriminately to corps composed of men of every description. The Soldiers in the Gorkha service are in general fine muscular men, their average height being about five feet, eight inches. They are little trammelled by the prejudices of caste and are in many respects decidedly superior to the British Sepoy. Under their present commander, they are subject to the most strict discipline and obey without a murmur any order emanating from his authority even to the extent of submitting cheerfully to privations in order to add to his pleasure, and as sentries their bearing is admirable. Although on the occasion of the Review at Kathmandhoo at least 6,000 men were under arms, only one Regiment (the Rifles) underwent an inspection. The manœuvres were very steadily performed, but it was evident that in Military parlance the corps was only practising a card, *i. e.*, going through a certain number of movements learnt by rote without comprehending in the slightest degree the occasions to which the different evolutions would be applicable, in fact the knowledge which they have acquired of the science of tactics is, I should suppose, sufficient to prove the truth of the old adage "that a little learning is a dangerous thing," as it is not unlikely should they ever again come in collision with our forces, that instead of carrying on a Guerilla warfare, the system best adapted both to their habits and the nature of their country, they would attempt to operate in masses, and consequently by becoming out-manœuvred lose all the advantage, which, from their courage and activity, they now have over our Native Troops. As tacticians the Gorkha Officers are certainly inferior to those of the late Seikh Army, and I doubt much whether there is one amongst them capable of moving a Brigade or even a Regiment anywhere but upon its own Parade ground. The Artillery attached to the Nepal Army numbers about 300 guns, of which 160 are retained at the Capital and the remainder mounted at the different fortresses and outposts. Those at Kathmandhoo are all in serviceable condition and well adapted for mountain warfare, being chiefly of small calibre, from 2 to 6-pounders,—they are worked by hand the prejudices of Hindoos, as respects the sacred animal, preventing their using bullocks for draught purposes whilst horses would not only be expensive but almost useless; the Government has lately made arrangements, by separating the gun from the carriage, for transporting field pieces by means of elephants, and from the capabilities of these animals to ascend and descend paths which would appear almost impassable to any but a highland pony, there is little doubt that this description of carriage would prove of the utmost utility in a hilly country.

Unlike the generality of Native Powers the Nepalese do not apparently attach much consideration to the practice of their Artillery, and it is therefore perhaps far inferior to that against which we have recently had to contend in our Indian campaigns. Their balls are chiefly of lead, as they are unable to cast iron, those made of the latter metal are beaten, and a single ball fully requires the labor of three men (whose wages amount to 5 annas each per diem) throughout the whole of one day, ere it is fit for use, thus (including the expense of charcoal) the average cost of making alone may be estimated at a rupee; their shells are, I presume, of pewter. They are in a great measure unacquainted with the art of manufacturing fuzes, General Jung Bahadur has devoted much time and attention towards making experiments in order to ascertain the exact proportions of the ingredients used in preparing the composition, but hitherto with but little success; whatever information they may have acquired, as to the course of study to be pursued in the Laboratory School to render an Artillery-man duly efficient, has in all probability been derived from French Officers, two of whom I am led to believe received service in Nepal subsequent to the ratification of the present treaty with the British.

There is a foundry at Kathmandhoo and a large manufactory of fire arms at Peutana, about 15 marches distant. The guns are of brass, (copper and zinc,) and bored by machinery worked by water power; in preparing the castings, the moulds are placed at a considerable interval from the furnace, and the molten liquid instead of being conducted to the former by means of a gutter, is conveyed in small earthen pots, thus the gun is as it were formed in layers and little allowance being made for dead head, none of the impurities existing in the metal are removed, and it must consequently be liable to flaws, although not to the extent that would occur in one of our guns, which are of bronze, thus cast. The rifles and muskets in use with the Gorkha Army are of fair construction, but with rude flint locks, a few are now made upon the percussion principle, but as the manufacture of caps is not likely to be introduced into Nepal, they cannot become general. The bayonets are for the most part shaped like the Gorkha knife, being broad and flat with a slight curve : they appear serviceable weapons and are alike available for cut or thrust. The three principal Magazines in Nepal are situated at Kathmandhoo, Bhatgaon and Peutana. The former contains about 25,000 stand of arms, the greater number in wretched order, it is supposed that in case of emergency, the Government could supply muskets and accoutrements sufficient to equip upwards of 100,000 men.

When on parade, the troops wear red coats and dark pantaloons of English material and pattern, but on all other duties the native mirzai of blue quilted cotton with loose white paejamahs or dhotics is the costume adopted, their equipments are of a very inferior description.

As an aggressive foe, I should consider the Gorkhas, although a brave and warlike race, if not contemptible at least little to be dreaded; no Commissariat is attached to their army, and when on the march each Soldier carries his own provisions for the number of days he is likely to be absent, an arrangement which may answer for an ordinary move through friendly territories, or even for a detachment engaged in a foray into an enemy's country, but is perfectly impracticable for a large force employed upon a protracted campaign; for it cannot be disputed that when troops are under the necessity of operating in masses exposed to the attack of a skilful opponent, even the most successful foragers, must, in some measure, be dependent on an organized department for the provision of supplies, more especially when as in the case of the Gorkha army, they would have to oppose an enemy powerful in Cavalry, whilst themselves not only weak in that arm but actually unable to command the services of a single horseman, without referring to our early wars in India or to the history of the Peninsular Campaign to adduce proof in support of this assertion, I may mention that in 1845-46, previous to the Battle of Sobraon, the Seikh troops then posted on the Sutledge suffered from scarcity in their camp, although numbering a large force of Cavalry, and with the whole of the resources of the Punjaub at their disposal, how much more then would this rule apply, to an army commanded by Generals unskilled in direeting the movements of large bodies and marching through an enemy's Provinees, surrounded by hostile Cavalry, against which it would be out of their powcr to oppose a corresponding foree; it may be admitted that for a short period they would be able to subsist by the plunder of the different villages through whieh their route might be direeted, but their progrcss would neeessarily be slow, as not only are the Soldiers like all inhabitants of mountainous countries bad walkers in the plains, their average rate of marehing little exceeding two miles per hour, but supposing they deseended by any of the passes leading into the Gorukhpore, Chumparun or Tirhoot distriets, in whatever direction they might move, they would find their route interseeted by Rivers such as the Gunduk, Gograh, Raptee and numerous other streams of less importanee, aeross which, from my experience of their ineapacity, from want of method, for eonducting military operations of this nature, I feel justified in stating it would be a work of several days to transport a force of any magnitude; in the meantime they would be restricted to a very limited space for the collection of their supplies, and due precautions might be taken to prevent their enjoying the oppportunity of availing themselves of the resources of the country through which they would subsequently have to pass.

Another argument that might be advanced against the ability of the Nepal Army to engage in Foreign Warfare is the want of Camp Equipage. A very small number of tents, merely sufficient to accommodate the men actually on Guard, are issued to the troops, for the most part therefore they have only such shelter as may be afforded by temporary huts which they are extremely expert in constructing of boughs and grass, but they are pervious to rain, and moreover could only be prepared during a halt. Thus in the course of a campaign the soldiers would be fully exposed to the inclemency of the weather, and, as I believe the hill-men suffer even more than our own troops from such exposure when in the plains, after the heavy rain which is generally expected about the middle of the cold season, it may justly be inferred that an invading force would, owing to the prevalence of sickness, become considerably weakened if not rendered almost inefficient and obliged to effect a retreat.*

It must not be supposed that I am inclined to underrate the Gorkha power, far from it, I am truly persuaded the Nepalese would prove an active and enterprising enemy, and in the event of any supineness on the part of the Indian Government, at the commencement of hostilities would inflict serious injury on the Provinces bordering their territories, but from the causes mentioned above, it would be only necessary for us to take

* Several casualties occurred amongst General Jung Bahadur's suite, whilst we were encamped at Bissowleeah.

common precautionary measures for the purpose of strengthening our Frontier to prevent their ever seriously entertaining, or at all events carrying into execution, a project for the invasion of British India. By moving from the Meerut and Cawnpore Divisions a strong Brigade of Cavalry, including an European Corps, to the vicinity of Bettiah, advancing the Regiment of Irregulars, now at Sultanpore, and the Benares Battery to Gorukhpore, and reinforcing Almorah and Darjeeling, especially the latter, which would be the first point against which the Gorkhas would direct their attack, with Infantry and details of Artillery from Meerut and Dinapore; our territories would be fully protected from insult and the inroads of marauding parties effectually checked.

Should a *casus belli* ever again arise between the two Governments, in my humble opinion, unless political reasons dictated the expediency of the measure, it would be hardly advisable for our troops to attempt to penetrate into the interior of Nepal, as in order to ensure submission on the part of the Durbar, it would, in all probability, be merely necessary for us to take possession of the Terai land situated at the foot of the hills to the east of the Gunduk, ceded to the Gorkhas at the termination of the war in 1816, thus weakening the Government and to a certain extent starving the people, by depriving one of the possessions from which they now draw a very considerable amount of revenue, and the other of lands supplying a large portion of the grain required for their consumption. The value of the acquired territory would in a great degree, if not entirely, compensate us for the extra expense incurred in maintaining a respectable force on the Frontier during the months of November, December, January, February, and March; at which period alone our Provinces would be exposed to the incursions of Gorkha Troops, as throughout the remainder of the year the forest is almost impassable, owing to the deadly nature of the malaria, styled by the inhabitants the Oul, generated by the accumulation of dead vegetation throughout this immense tract of jungle. I have specified Cavalry as the force by which our Frontier should be principally held in the event of a rupture with the Nepalese, from the well-known dread which their troops entertain of that arm, owing to their utter inability, consequent on their imperfect formation, to resist a charge. This was particularly exemplified in the attack made during the last war by Lt. Pickersgill upon a party of Gorkha soldiers which he completely routed, and so great was the consternation thereby created amongst them, that they immediatly evacuated the whole of the lowlands, and retreated to the hills, although they had previously displayed the utmost daring and almost destroyed two of our detachments at Pursa and Summundpore under the command of Captains Sibley and Blackney; moreover the very fact of their being liable to be cut off in their retreat to their fastnesses would deter marauding parties from ravaging our villages along the borders of the Terai, whilst not only would they experience little dread of being overtaken by our Infantry, but it might be hazardous to detach a small body of that arm in pursuit of plunderers, from the danger of its being entrapped into an ambuscade, a design which would most probably be adopted by the Gorkhas, who, like all natives of the East, are adepts in practising *ruses de guerre*. To this risk it is obvious that horsemen would not be exposed, as, from the greater rapidity and duration of their movements, they would be enabled to pursue the enemy to the very edge of the jungle and at the same time encamp at such a distance from the forest as to preclude with ordinary precautions the possibility of their being surprised and overpowered in a night attack.

Supposing, that to avenge an insult and to vindicate our honor, it might be deemed imperative upon us to impose such stringent terms upon the Durbar as could only be demanded with any prospect of success after the utter defeat and prostration of their arms and the occupation of their capital by our troops, although a force might be assembled in Kemaon as a demonstration ready to take advantage of circumstances enabling us to push our operations in that quarter, and a light brigade formed at the sanitary station of Darjeeling for the purpose of effecting a diversion on the eastern frontier, where I believe a vulnerable point could be discovered with little difficulty; it is to be presumed that, as before, the principal attack would be directed on the valley of Kathmandhoo.

The route usually followed by merchants and travellers, and which may in fact be considered the grand highway to Nepal, is that *vià* Semul-Basa and Hetoundah; after entering the sal jungle at the former station, it becomes a mere track only available for horse or foot passengers and beasts of burthen, but, as throughout the first march (about 10 miles in length,) until you enter the bed of the Chiriya Khurree at Bicheeah Khor, it is almost perfectly level and passes through a fine forest with little or no underwood, it might be converted into a good road without much expenditure of labor. From Bicheeah Khor, where there is a village consisting of a brick house and a few huts, it follows the course of the river, during the cold season a trickling stream, never more than a few inches in depth and in many places entirely disappearing beneath the surface, its bed although in the first instance at least a quarter of a mile in breadth narrowing occasionally to about 150 yards and being throughout commanded by ridges of hills, averaging, I should suppose, some 300 feet in height, most of which it would be necessary to occupy before moving to the attack of the pass. About the 3rd mile the Iona

Nuddee emerges from the cliffs on the right hand and joins the Chiriya Khurree. I am induced to imagine that it must have been some where near this point that General Ochterlony diverged from the main path when he turned the Gorkha stockades on the Chiriya Ghati range on the 15th February 1816. One of the Nepal Sirdars alluded to the existence of a track branching off in the direction of the valley of Mukwanpore. From the commencement of the march there is a gradual ascent and the firs growing on the hills denote a change of temperature from that of the burning plains. The road is covered with boulders of sand, granite, schistose mica and pudding stone, but until the 6th mile where it enters the pass, it could with little difficulty be rendered practicable for wheel carriages, and the Ghat itself although at present extremely steep, and almost impassable for laden buffaloes, could, I am convinced, by the exertions of an experienced body of Sappers and Miners under the directions of a skilful Officer, be made available for the passage of Artillery, and even bullock carts. It is very narrow and the hills, covered with brush-wood, rise to the right and left almost perpendicularly; on the north side the descent is abrupt and terminates in the channel of another hill stream the Kuhrua, which the path follows for about a mile when it turns to the right, and now skirting, now penetrating the forest, after traversing a succession of undulations reaches Hetoundah without encountering any irregularity of ground or other material obstacle which might prove a bar either to the movements of an army or the operations of traffic. About a mile from the village it crosses the Khurra Nuddee, a shallow stream, across which a light wooden bridge has lately been thrown, the abutments being of masonry with the flooring composed of layers of beams five or six in number at each extremity and gradually tapering towards the centre, which only consists of a single plank.

Besides the road described in the preceding paragraph there is another *viâ* Jugulpore, Ruttunpore and Hurryhurpore by which Hetoundah can be approached; it is now seldom used, but is said for the greater part of the distance to be perfectly practicable for hackeries; it traverses for several miles the bed of the Lukhundie Nuddee.

Hetoundah is situated on the Raptee, it is a great emporium for trade, contains a large Dhurm Sala for the reception of travellers, and during the cold season is a considerable village, but being considered one of the most unhealthy spots in the Terai, from April to November is almost deserted. In the vicinity there is some attempt at cultivation which would doubtless be extended were the Nepal Government to sanction the jungle being cleared, but they evidently consider this their most formidable defence against an invasion undertaken by British Troops. This would prove a most important station to an invading army, as here they would be enabled to collect cattle and supplies previous to the advance on the capital, and from this point two routes lead into the valley of Kathmandhoo, the one *viâ* Mukwanpore and the other by Bheem Phédee and Seesa Gurhee, the latter is the track generally pursued by Europeans and which alone I am able to describe from personal observation. For the first 14 miles it follows the course of the Raptee, a stream everywhere fordable in the cold season, but in the rains in all probability a furious torrent; this river it crosses about twenty times by temporary bridges composed of heaps of loose stones as piers, with a flooring of brushwood and sods. The road is, at present, wretched, but perfectly susceptible at a very trifling expense of being made a fair route, save for wheel carriages, in many places merely requiring a few blows of the axe to remove the branches which now impede the traveller's progress; throughout the whole distance, it lies between ranges of steep hills, covered for the most part, with heavy tree jungle; but except at one or two points, troops moving by it, would be little exposed to the fire of an enemy crowning the heights. About the 8th mile is situated the village of Maha Paka, it is stated by Hamilton, that a path leads hence over the Seesa Panee mountains to the Panauni. At Dhokha Phédee, the route leaves the water-shed and turning slightly to the left through a narrow pass ascends a piece of table land situated between a broad water course and the river, still, however, overlooked, although from their great distance, not commanded by the neighbouring mountains; here and there are little patches of cultivation which extend as far as Bheem Phédee the 3rd stage in the Terai, (about 18 miles from Hetoundah) where there is an open space with a small village and Dhurm Sala, but only one spring; this locality is at some degree of elevation and supposed to be free from the malaria which pervades the lower tracts.

At Bheem Phédee the ordinary traveller leaves his gallant steed and continues his journey in a dandee, or hammock swung upon a single pole, and carried by 4 or 2 men as the breadth of the path may admit. The road takes a westerly direction and abruptly faces the mountain of Seesa Panee. At about the distance of two miles and perpendicular height of five hundred and thirty yards, it passes the fort, once considered one of the bulwarks of the country and beyond which no stranger can penetrate without an order from the Prime Minister. It is at present in bad repair, and except from its commanding position which renders it difficult of access, claims, in a Military point of view, but little attention.

The following extract from my journal, written whilst the scenes I traversed were still fresh in my memory, may perhaps give a better description of the route from Bheem Phédee to Pheer Phing than any that

I could now record, although it was noted more as a Tourist than a Soldier:—"About 11 A. M. started from Bheem Phédee, the view as we ascended was extremely lovely; the valley below us appearing dotted with patches of verdure, coming out under the bright sunshine in bold relief to the sombre cliffs, which, with their masses of dark foliage, encompassed us in every direction, whilst the course of the Raptee seemed as a broad road winding through the woods until lost to sight far in the distance; the cottages perched here and there having a most picturesque appearance, the height at which we were, preventing the squalor and wretchedness with which they were environed being visible. Ere, however, we reached the fort of Seesa Gurhee, we were surrounded by mist, and the clouds acting as a curtain, hid the adjacent scenery from our eyes. At Seesa Gurhee there is a detachment of Gorkha troops. The fort seemed contemptible, and would, I should imagine, offer but a feeble resistance to an invading army. The whole side of the hill, although steep, is not inaccessible, and could, I firmly believe, in many places, be scaled by daring light troops. The road, in fact owes little to science being a mere track apparently worn by travellers, and yet it is traversed not only by the hill coolies carrying immense weights in baskets, shaped like semi-truncated cones, suspended from their backs by a broad band passing round their foreheads; but also by lightly laden elephants, and horsemen mounted on the ponies peculiar to the country. It improves after passing the fort, and ascending nearly another mile crosses the summit of the range and winds down through dense forests to the channel of the Panauni; which whilst we were still several hundred feet above it, was disclosed to our view wending its tortuous course through mountains about 2000 feet in height. This stream we crossed five times, once by a wooden bridge of the same description as that thrown across the Khurra Nuddee, we then left the main road, such as it is, and turning sharp to our right ascended the hill by a path in some places almost perpendicular, and so narrow, that lying in my dandee, I felt myself actually suspended over the precipices below. Here also the view was superb, the Chundra Geree mountain, surmounted by the stupendous Himalayas capped with snow and tinged by the rays of the declining sun, stretching out boldly to our front, whilst below us were seen hamlets and fields reminding one, from the peculiar freshness of the verdure, of scenes in our native land. After crossing the summit of this range we commenced a series of almost innumerable ascents and descents, now plunging into the dark recesses of a forest glade, now following the course of some purling stream, until, when still far from our destination, night cast its shadows around us, and we were glad to seek refuge by the fire of a detachment of Gorkha soldiers, who kindly made way for us; one of their number charitably allowing me the use of a portion of his blanket to lie upon; here we remained for about half an hour, when men with torches who had been despatched by Jung Bahadur to meet us arrived, and we continued our journey. After traversing two more ranges of hills and crossing the same number of streams we reached Pheer Phing, it was too dark to remark the road, but in many places I noticed that it was bounded by cactus hedges. Pheer Phing seemed a town containing about 2,000 inhabitants, it is built much in the Chinese fashion; the Minister was residing in a building apparently on the outskirts; he was delighted to see us, saying that he had suffered much anxiety on our account, we were ushered into a room where a large dinner had been prepared, of which we were glad to partake, having eaten nothing exeept a crust of bread since 4 A. M. Being now in the valley of Nepal, we were able to proceed in palkees which were in readiness for us. Started about 11 P. M. and arrived at the Residency at 3 in the morning." The route above described, is not the one usually pursued by persons travelling viâ Pheer Phing, which does not bend to the right for at least a mile above the point where we ascended the mountain range. It is. far easier and consequently generally adopted by merchants in preference to the more direct road over the Chundra Geree pass from which it diverges at the foot of the Ekdunta hill. By this way passengers encounter no obstruction of any moment, and the journey can be accomplished by horsemen with the utmost facility. From Tamba Khani, a village situated at the foot of the Seesa Panee Hill on the north side, which evidently derives its name from its vicinity to some copper mines, now, I believe, closed, the distance to Kathmandhoo by the main path is considered to be 23 miles, whilst I am convinced we did not at the utmost save more than 2 miles by following the far more difficult, and in fact, almost dangerous track.

I have alluded to a direct road from Tamba Khani to Kathmandhoo by which the journey is reduced to 19 miles; it follows the bed of the Panauni river, which it crosses several times, as far as Makoo, here it ascends rather a steep hill, and subsequently by a succession of gentle undulations continues its course along the slope of a range of heights to the left, passing about the 7th mile the village of Chitlong, where there is a bazar and a few brick houses, and soon after commences the ascent of the Chundra Geree pass, the summit of which, if I recollect right, is about 9,000 feet above the level of the sea, and is often covered with snow; the rise on the southern side is very gradual and could be surmounted without much difficulty even by equestrians, the slope is covered with trees and bushes but no underwood; the descent into the valley of Kathmandhoo is extremely precipitous and guns could only be taken down piecemeal, the hamlet of Than Kot is situated at the foot, and thence to the capital there is a very fair road which could be made practicable for Artillery, in fact from the moment an invading army accomplishes the passage of the Chundra Geree pass, no other serious natural obstacle exists to its march on Kathmandhoo, that is, during the season in which Military operations are carried on, when all the hill streams are fordable; during the rains it is only natural to suppose that several of them would become almost impassable.

From Chitlong another road branches off to Kathmandhoo running over the Doona Baisea mountain, and this was the track pursued by the British Mission in 1793, but as it causes a detour of upwards of 30 miles, the distance being about 45, whilst by Than Kot it is only 11, and apparently the country through which it lies, is equally rugged and precipitous as that to be encountered on the more direct route, no object would be gained by adopting it, moreover it would be dangerous in a mountainous country to march a detached division or brigade upon a road by which they might be so completely separated and liable to be cut off from the main body; for Military purposes, it may therefore be deemed useless.

I have already mentioned that from the village of Hetoundah, two routes lead to the valley of Kathmandhoo, the second for the first few miles follows the course of the Khurra Nuddee and crosses the mountain range at Mukwanpore, it is that on which the victorious column under General Ochterlony was directed during the Nepal war in 1816, and is stated by Colonel Kirkpatrick to be the one by which intercourse is maintained between Nepal and the

Terai during the rainy season when that by the valley of the Raptee becomes impracticable, even during the rest of the year, it appears to be preferred by the Natives of the country and consequently may be fairly conceived to be the most easy and expeditious. The fort of Mukwanpore is situated on a high hill about five miles to the Eastward of Hetoundah and is apparently the key of the passage, as in the Adjutant General's letter, dated 6th November 1814, no less than three roads are mentioned as diverging from this point, one by the way of Boorhan Choura and Phoolbaree, effecting a junction with the Chitlong road at Bheem Phédee, this is not, however, considered practicable for cattle. The second passes the village and ghaut of Nundrama Mahadeo communicating with Pheer Phing and is deemed less difficult. The third proceeds in an Easterly direction to Panus and Ambus, where by an inclination to the Northward it falls upon the Bhagmuttee at

Tansen, it is reported as being comparatively easy and perfectly accessible to cattle of all descriptions with the exception of camels. The distance from Mukwanpore to Pheer Phing is estimated at 14¾ coss and to Tansen 13 coss.

In addition to the routes above specified the three following are alluded to in the Blue Book published relative to the Nepal war. 1*st*.—From Bejapore in the Morung by the valley of the Kousee Nuddee.* 2*nd*.—By that of the Bhagmuttee which is supposed to be extremely easy and consequently jealously concealed by the Government, the channel forms the road and in the dry season the quantity of water must be trifling. 3*rd*.—Through Bootwul and Palpa this might perhaps be gained by in the first instance pursuing the course of the Gunduk River. A fourth road is that from Durbungah by the bed of the Comla

* Followed for a considerable distance by a Brigade under Col. Gregory in 1815.

River passing through Peperowa, Janikpore and Conlabaree. Near the latter place is the Fort of Seedlee taken by Capt. Kinloch who pursued this route in 1765. I have little doubt that full information relative to all the paths, which traverse the different mountain ranges dividing the plains of India from Nepal, could be easily obtained either from the refugees residing in our territories and who are naturally averse to the present administration, or from individuals of the Newar caste, especially the Kusāis, who are brought more into contact with the British than any other class, being employed in carrying the dandees in which the gentlemen of the Residency travel, and have evidently a very high idea of our wealth and generosity. At the same time I see no prospect of a rising in our favor, on the contrary, Col. Thoresby who was for many years Resident at the Court of Kathmandhoo, and well acquainted with the feelings of the people, assured me, that, in his opinion, we should be opposed by every male capable of bearing arms.

By whichever route our columns might be put in motion, wheel carriages could be but little used. Elephants, bullocks, mules and coolies would, therefore, be required in large numbers, as the whole of the grain, &c., necessary for the consumption of the troops, would have to be brought up from the plains; the hill coolies being accustomed to the country, can carry far greater weights than the Hindustanis; but, it is doubtful, whether their services could be secured, and we should, therefore, in all probability, be necessitated to depend upon those of our own Provinces.

The Nepalese carry their ammunition on men's backs, in oblong shallow wooden boxes, secured by leathern straps, many of which I noticed in their magazine; this is a plan we should be obliged to adopt; we should also be forced to exchange the doolies, now in use with our corps, for hill dandees. If I mistake not, a hammock, very similar to the latter article, has been invented by Dr. Login, which could be made available for all situations.

The camp equipage, for all ranks, would require to be on the most limited scale, and the whole of the heavy baggage should be left at the edge of the forest so that the column might march with as few incumbrances as possible. No inconvenience would be experienced from this arrangement, as during the cold season, little risk would be run from exposure to the climate, and the necessary supplies could be always furnished from the rear.

Of the ultimate success of our Arms over the Gorkha troops, even amongst their native mountains, there can, I imagine, be no doubt, and the Sirdars themselves have apparently but one opinion on the subject; still the campaign would be arduous and the struggle severe, and for the welfare of both States, it is sincerely to be hoped, it may never occur. Little benefit would accrue to England from the conquest of Nepal, whilst by cultivating her friendship, a route may perhaps be opened by which our commerce could be extended to the very heart of China and Thibet and the blessings of civilization placed within the reach of thousands of our fellow men.

Having now concluded the first portion of my task, I purpose offering an account of the Civil Institutions of Nepal, which however, owing to the limited period, eight days, of my stay at Kathmandhoo, will not prove as full and perfect as I could have wished.

CHAPTER II.

Government of Nepal—Prime Minister—His present position—Just measures—Influence—Raj Guru—Dhurm Adhikari—Civil Functionaries—Kazis—Dithas—Bicharis—Subahs—The Terai—Administration of Justice—Civil Courts—Legal Code—Political relations of the Court of Kathmandhoo—Chinese Embassy—Seikh Prisoners—Revenues of Nepal—Elephant catching—Mineral wealth—Coinage, Customs—Exports and Imports—Commerce—Traffic between British India and Thibet.

THE State of Nepal is nominally ruled by a Rajah; but even as far back as 1793, when the first British Mission entered the country, the kingly authority appears to have been, in a great measure, controlled by the Chief Councillor, whose power was again kept in check by the influence of the Members of the Bharadhar or Grand

Council, which, however, seems to have been exerted more to maintain the immunities and privileges of their own order than to ensure the due administration of justice and an equitable regard to the rights of the people at large, who, consequently, derived little advantage from the interposition of this barrier between themselves and the despotic authority which would otherwise have been exercised either by the monarch or his principal adviser.

Subsequent to the massacre of the Kot in 1846, when almost every Sirdar of note was either assassinated or forced to seek refuge in the British Territories, and an account of which shall be detailed in another Chapter, General Jung Bahadur, by his talents and determination, for there appears to have been but little display of gallantry, raised himself to the office of Prime Minister, and, owing to the pusillanimity or incapacity of the reigning monarch, has gradually usurped all the prerogatives of royalty.

*

Although outwardly all due respect is shown to the mandates of the Maha Rajah, Jung Bahadur has virtually assumed the reins of Government, and obeys merely the dictates of his own will, at the same time, however, it is obvious that he attaches a certain degree of importance to his Sovereign's favor and to his sanction of any measure which he may feel anxious to introduce, and would consequently have some little hesitation in acting in direct opposition to his wishes; still should a rupture ever occur he would not scruple to depose him, and in all probability place on the throne his infant son, by the Rani whose demise took place in October 1850, and whose memory he reveres, in consideration of the obligations which he acknowledges he often experienced from her during the first portion of his career as Premier.

All written and verbal communications, relative to affairs, Political, Fiscal and Judicial, are submitted to the Minister, who generally proceeds to issue his orders thereon, without in any way consulting either the opinion of the Maha Raja or that of the Grand Council, in fact, although Kazis and Officers of rank are still eligible to become members of the latter, and to be summoned to give their advice in matters of importance, when the exigencies of the State may demand it, the assembly is seldom convened and has little influence.

The minute supervision exercised by General Jung Bahadur over the management of all departments of the State is most extraordinary and deserving of the greatest commendation, for the amount of labor thereby entailed upon him must be immense. I believe, I am fully justified in saying that not a rupee is expended from the Public Treasury, nor a merchant permitted to pass the Forts at Mukwanpore or Seesa Gurhee without his knowledge and sanction. All appointments, Civil or Military, are conferred by the Minister, and all complaints regarding the conduct of Public Officials are brought to his notice and invariably meet with the utmost attention; and in cases where injustice has been committed, the complainant obtains immediate redress. This, I am able to assert from personal knowledge as respects the following instances. When encamped at Bissowleeah, one morning, as we were in the act of starting on a shooting excursion, General Jung Bahadur's elephant was surrounded by peasantry, clamouring loudly for justice and accusing the Subah of the district of oppression and tyranny. The Minister desired them to have patience, stating that he could not at that moment attend to their petition, but that their wrongs should be carefully enquired into and redressed. The following day an excuse, on the plea of public business, was sent for not joining our party; before night the charge brought against the Sirdar was proved, and notwithstanding the great influence of his family with the Minister, his brother being a most confidential Officer and one of those who accompanied the mission to England, he was removed from his appointment and directed to be imprisoned until he should repay the amount of his unjust exactions, and this sentence was immediately carried into effect. The second case was that of an Officer in charge of a district, who having on the part of Government rented a piece of land at a certain rate to one of the peasantry, subsequently received a higher offer from another party, which he accepted. The original applicant protested against this arrangement, but a deaf ear was turned to his petition. He appealed to the Supreme Court at Kathmandhoo, not only was a decision given in his favor, but the Sirdar fined 50 rupees for committing what was deemed an act of injustice; a short time after, the peasant had occasion to appear before him and was insolently rebuked for his presumption in preferring his complaint before the higher tribunal, a not perhaps over-respectful answer was given, the Officer became enraged and in his passion struck the man, who died from the effects of the blow. Although the Minister had the greatest esteem for the Sirdar and he was one of his principal supporters, he was deprived of his commission and subjected to close confinement where he may remain for years, if not for life.

From every quarter in which I have made enquiries, I have received favorable accounts of Jung Bahadur's administration. Formerly the people were treated almost like serfs by the oligarchy, who, as members of the Grand Council, superintended all affairs of State and in general retained the government of the kingdom completely in their own hands; now, on the contrary, the lowest peasant is not debarred from demanding justice, whatever may be the rank of the party against whom his complaint is urged, and consequently putting aside the feelings of a few of the Sirdars whose power he has curbed or whose ambition he has checked, the Minister is decidedly a popular Ruler.

The Raj Guru, or spiritual adviser to the Monarch, is an Official whose rank and influence may be considered as second only to that of the Minister; in fact, the latter even deems it politic to pay the greatest respect, on all occasions, to this dignitary of the church, and doubtless to this outward deference to one, who, as a Brahman of high caste and Chief Priest, must necessarily be regarded with reverence by a very large portion of the population, he owes much of his own power. On the occasion of the return of the Mission from England, the Guru was induced, by the offer of handsome presents, to leave Nepal for the purpose of attending the different religious ceremonies observed on the banks of the Ganges at Benares, and thus the protecting mantle of his sanctity being flung over those who had accomplished the journey to the land of the infidel; not even the most bigoted and orthodox Hindu could presume to cavil or express doubts as to their entire purification.

The Guru presides over the Court, styled Dhurm Adhikari, in which he expounds the Shastr and takes cognizance of all offences committed contrary to the precepts inculcated in the holy writings: he is entitled to the fines levied on the perpetration of certain transgressions, for instance, if a cow dies or is killed within a house, having a rope round her neck, the owner, ere he can regain his caste, must perform penance and pay a heavy penalty as an atonement for having bound the sacred animal. A person who may eat rice or dāl without taking off certain articles of dress, is also liable to the same punishment. Colonel Kirkpatrick states that maltreatment, of any kind, of a cow, subjects the offender to the payment of a fine, and I should think this certainly most probable.

Amongst Civil Functionaries the highest rank is that of Kazi; no special duties, however, appear to be attached to this dignity, and Kazis may be indiscriminately employed either as Judicial Officers, or as Sirdars entrusted with the general superintendence of certain districts, and having irregular troops under their command; they are all, as before mentioned, eligible to seats in the Grand Council whenever it may be assembled, and also liable to be summoned to assist at the investigation of serious cases at either of the principal Courts at the Capital.

Kirkpatrick mentions that there were only 4 Kazis in Office at the period he visited Nepal, but at the present time I conceive, that there is no prescribed limit to their number, which is entirely regulated by the will or judgment of the Minister.

There are two grades of Judicial or rather Magisterial Officers styled Dithas and Bicharis, the former take cognizance of offences of a serious nature and their individual jurisdiction extends over several districts. They are empowered to adjudge as a punishment, confinement, for periods not exceeding a month, or to amerce delinquents in sums as high as 500 rupees. All crimes rendering the guilty parties subject to mutilation or death must, however, be submitted for the decision of the higher tribunals at the Capital. Bicharis are appointed to every district, and their powers are limited to investigating cases of a trivial nature, levying fines of 100 rupees and awarding sentences of imprisonment for a term of not more than a few days' duration.

Fiscal Officers, styled Subahs, are attached to Provinces. Occasionally they farm the Revenue from Government, but, as a general rule, they may be considered as Collectors on the part of the State, they are, I believe, sometimes invested with magisterial authority.

The Terai is apparently what may be called a Non-Regulation Province, governed by an Officer of rank having under his orders a Sirdar and several Subahs, it is the duty of the former to take notice of, and investigate, all offences either Civil or Criminal, which may be committed throughout the whole of the lowlands, forwarding the necessary depositions to the Governor, who, except in cases involving forfeiture of life or limb, which are submitted for the orders of the Minister, adjudicates thereon, and his decree is deemed final. The Subahs, as in Nepal, are either Farmers or Collcetors of the Revenue ; their accounts being supervised by the Governor, who is responsible to the Durbar for due preeautions being observed to prevent the occurrence of fraud and defalcation, which, however, eonsequent on the proximity of our territories, in which the delinquent generally seeks refuge with his ill-gotten wealth, not unfrequently takes place. The present Governor of the Terai is General Krishna Bahadur, a younger brother of the Minister;

his residence is at Khutta Bunga where the Head-Quarters of two Corps the Shere and Subz Dul are stationed. The tribunals for the administration of justice at Kathmandhoo are the Eta Chaplee, Kothee, Ling, Tuksal, and Dhunsar; the two former are the principal Civil and Criminal Courts and presided over by a Sirdar, the latter are each composed of two Bicharis. There is another Court styled the Kewaree Chauk, which is rather an office of Audit, where a general supervision is exercised over the accounts of the Subahs, than a place of judicature. The President of this assembly is sometimes a Military Officer, the office was formerly held by General Budreena Sing, who was removed in consequence of his being implicated in the recent conspiracy against General Jung Bahadur.

The Dhurma Shastr forms the basis of the Civil and Criminal jurisprudence of Nepal, the expounder in all intricate cases being, as already stated, the Raj Guru. Of the Civil department, it is out of my power to express any opinion, but I believe it is not very inferior and, in some respects, probably, is even preferable to the systems in force in far more civilized countries, where the glorious uncertainty of the law has become a proverb and its delays a by-word.

The Criminal branch is administered with energy, and consequently theft is a crime that rarely occurs. During my march with the Mission to Kathmandhoo, although from the moment we crossed the border not the slightest precaution was taken to guard against robbery, I did not hear of a single case throughout a Camp containing 6 or 7,000 persons.

Trial by ordeal is sanctioned and often practised. It is conducted by the test of water, and I understand the proceedings are similar to those in vogue in other Hindu States. As the special object of the Nepalese Courts is to ensure the punishment and prevention of crime, every measure calculated to secure conviction is used without scruple, and little attention is paid to legal technicalities. A criminal can be found guilty merely on his own evidence, and, in fact, to enable the judge to award sentence, it is considered absolutely necessary that the culprit should acknowledge his guilt.

The Code of Laws formerly administered in Nepal has been much modified and rendered more lenient by the present Minister; the undermentioned crimes alone are now punishable by death,—murder, treason against the King or Prime Minister, attacks upon the persons of the British or Chinese Envoys, and theft in the third instance, in the first flogging, and in the second amputation of the arm, being awarded. The other penalties prescribed for different offences are confiscation of property, banishment, degradation from caste, imprisonment, and the imposition of fines; the three former are however now seldom inflicted. Incest is punished by emasculation, adultery is commonly revenged by the party offended against, who is allowed to vindicate his honor without the interference of the police; women for this offence are liable to have their lips and noses cut off, but I suspect that the nature of their punishment generally depends much upon their own caste and that of the person with whom they have intrigued. The sentence of death cannot be awarded against any member of the fair sex, whatever may have been the crime of which she has been found culpable: women are however subject to other very severe punishments, mutilation being the most common. Gambling is prohibited in Nepal, and, except during the Dewali, when there is no restriction and for five days the vice is universally indulged in, any infringement of this law is severely punished.

The Court of Nepal maintains Political relations both with England and China. Every fifth year a Mission is despatched from Kathmandhoo with presents for the

Emperor at Pekin. It always consists of 27 persons, as in the event of any variation taking place in the number, it would not be received by the Chinese authorities; it must also invariably arrive on the Frontier on the same day, and have under its charge exactly the same articles, as originally prescribed by the Treaty of 1792, not the slightest deviation from the rules then dictated being allowed, no plea even would be admitted for making any alteration either in the dates or stages, as directed for its route to, and from, the capital; with this exception the Mission experiences favorable treatment. An officer of Rank with an Escort is appointed to accompany it, and he is responsible for the Members being supplied, at the expense of his own Goverment, with every thing which may conduce to their comfort. To such an extent is this complaisance carried, that even the gratification of their sensual desires is not forgotten, and arrangements made accordingly; at the same time should one of their number be in a dying state, he would not be allowed to halt, but in the event of a palankeen not being available, which is the case for some part of the way, he would be tied on to his saddle and compelled to continue his journey.

The Mission is absent from Nepal 18 months, and remains 45 days at Pekin, during which period the superior Officers, on five or six occasions, are admitted to an audience with the Emperor. During the interview, having in the first instance made the three prostrations of the body (Kao tao), they are obliged to remain in a kneeling posture, this is, in accordance with Court etiquette, no one being permitted to stand in the Royal presence. As it is not deemed requisite that cushions should be supplied to the Chinese Ministers whilst in attendance on their Sovereign, each individual, when proceeding to the Palace, carries under his arm a small carpet, which he spreads before him on entering the room in which His Majesty is sitting.

Pekin is described by the Sirdars, who have accompanied the Mission, as a fine town, but the buildings are chiefly only one story in height.

Occasionally an Envoy from the Great Lama at Thibet makes his appearance at Kathmandhoo, but although his visit is doubtless sanctioned by the Chinese Government, and should it be necessary he would act in a political capacity, he cannot be considered as an accredited Agent; his ostensible duty is to inspect the Budhist temples in the vicinity of the City. There is a Nepalese Agent at Lassa to watch over the interests of the Newars engaged in commerce who reside at that City.

Although presents are transmitted to Kathmandhoo in return for those offered to the Emperor, there can be but little doubt that the latter are considered in the light of tribute from a dependant State and not as marks of esteem from an equal power, the Nepalese naturally repudiate this idea, but still they cannot deny, that the quinquennial Mission is one of the conditions imposed by the vietorious Chinese General when encamped at Nyakot, almost within sight of Kathmandhoo; with regard to the policy of the Nepal Durbar in thus ineurring the humiliation of suing for an ignominious peaee, there are various opinions, Colonel Kirkpatrick who visited the country almost immediately after the signing of the treaty, states, that the necessity for the measure was doubtful, as the invading army suffered from disease and searcity, and would soon have been eompelled to solicit the terms which they made a merit of granting. From all I could glean it would appear that hostilities were commeneed by the Gorkhas, who entered the Chinese territories, and on their return, loaded with plunder but with little provision, were attacked and defeated by an overwhelming foree of Tartars. According to Gorkha traditions extreme hardships from exposure and hunger were endured by their troops on this expedition, to such an extent indeed, as to have completely deterred them from ever again making incursions, in that direction, beyond their own Frontier. The dread formerly entertained of Tartar troops has, I have reason to believe, now quite subsided, and, for some time past, the Durbar have been casting longing eyes on one or two of the small States adjoining their territories but tributary to China, unless, however, aided by the resources of the Indian Government, regarding which arrangement I have often heard hints offered; the want of an efficient Commissariat Department would alone prove an obstacle to their moving a large body of troops in that quarter.

When the Seikh force under Zorawur Sing, which attempted to penetrate into Thibet by the Cashmere route, was defeated by the Tartars, four or five hundred men were taken prisoners and carried into captivity near the Gorkha Frontier, where some of them still exist; a letter was despatched by the Durbar to the Emperor soliciting their release, of this Missive not the slightest notice was ever accorded, a tolerable proof of the estimation in which the Nepal Ruler is held by his Imperial Majesty.

To a Hindú Nation, a constrained Mission to an infidel country where little regard is paid to their prejudices, must, it is evident, be considered in the light of a national disgrace, indeed, all the Members are deemed so completely to have lost caste during their journey, that on their return they are obliged to halt for 3 days at Nyakot, 18 miles from the capital, in order to perform certain religious ceremonies as a purification, and even then it is thought necessary, to prevent their being reproached with having forfeited their religious rights, that the Rajah should present them with water out of his own lota, as an acknowledgment of their having been re-admitted into the pale of the church.

Of the revenues of Nepal, I regret to state, it is out of my power to afford any certain information. I doubt, in fact, whether an accurate statement could be framed even from the records possessed by the Durbar, as the Civil and Military Establishments being paid almost entirely by Jagirs, or assignments of land, the sums actually realized at the Public Treasury must be far less than the real value of the land-tax, which forms the most considerable item in their accounts, whilst at the same time it is probable, that in the register of Jagirs, the worth of each allotment is greatly exaggerated, or at all events rated at the highest value, without reference to the depreciation in rents which must occasionally occur owing to drought or other causes. Colonel Kirkpatrick estimated the total amount received by the Government at from 25 to 30 lacs, but I am inclined to believe that it has materially increased within the present century, and may now be justly calculated as, at the least, 50 lacs. During the last few years a considerable augmentation has taken place in the Revenue derived from the Terai, owing, doubtless, to the minute supervision and admirable management of the present Minister. When ceded to the Gorkhas in 1816, this district was valued at only 2 or 3 lacs, whilst I have ascertained from several quarters that it yields nearly 20. This sum is collected principally from the land-tax, but this is not the only source; about 3 lacs per annum is paid by contractors for the privilege of cutting timber in the forest; and the jungle is also let for grazing, 4 annas per head being levied on buffaloes or black cattle, cows are allowed free pasturage; large herds annually enter the Terai from the British Provinces, and as the casualties are numerous, a flourishing trade is carried on in hides by speculators, residing on the borders, who forward them by water to the Calcutta market. Another item in the receipts is the profits obtained from elephant catching; in 1850 the number caught was certainly 200, and although many of them were small, I should hardly think their average value less than 300 rupees, thus, allowing 10,000 rupees on account of expenditure for establishments, the total amount cleared would be 50,000 rupees, and I suppose this may be considered as a tolerable approximation to the usual annual rate.

There are two modes adopted in Nepal for seizing wild elephants, the one either by pits or keddahs (enclosures) as practised in Hindustan, and the other by hunting them by means of tame ones; the latter is the most exciting, fatiguing, and dangerous sport I have ever witnessed; the wild elephants are in the first instance driven by beaters (regiments being frequently employed for this purpose) towards some well-known pass, at the extremity of which the huntsmen are stationed; as the breaking of the boughs in the forest and the shots and shouts of the pursuers denote the rapid approach of the herd, the utmost anxiety appears depicted in every countenance, and strange to say even the tame elephants remain motionless, fearing lest they should betray their position and scare their wild brethren, ere the cordon gradually closing round them has been properly formed; at last the signal is given, and perhaps 30 or 40 elephants rush forward, crushing the thick jungle and trampling down the high grass beneath their feet. As soon as the wild animals are seen, one is separated from its companions and closely followed by the hunters; the danger now commences, for not only is there a chance of being attacked by the hunted elephant, but the utmost agility is required to prevent being killed by coming in contact with the branches or stems of the trees through which you urge your course. Howdahs would be useless, as in a few minutes they would be smashed to atoms. The sportsman therefore maintains his seat merely by the aid of a rope attached to a very small pad on the elephant's back and having a noose through which the hand is passed; he must trust entirely to his own presence of mind and activity, to escape the dangers that threaten him, now springing to the right, now to the left, at one moment standing almost erect, and spurring on his ungainly courser with a mallet, in which a spike is affixed, which he holds in the left hand, the next seeking shelter from some impending bough behind the animal's tail. The pace at which the chase is kept up is almost 8 miles an hour, and it may continue for 30 or 40 minutes, sometimes much longer. Any one therefore, who has ever mounted an elephant, may form some idea of the exertion which has to be undergone; at last the wild beast is surrounded by the tame ones, and whilst being regularly jostled, some skilful mahout flings, with the aid of his elephant, a rope round its neck by which it is soon securely fastened, and placed under charge of two others, selected for their size and power, whilst the captors turn back to seek another victim. In this way three or four are caught in a single day. They are so effectually subdued by hunger and the dread of their powerful guardians, who treat them most unmercifully, that occasionally at the expiration of three days from the date of their being seized, they may be seen with riders on their backs. When a wild elephant is what is termed Must, or mad, it is extremely hazardous to approach him, as instead of flying he would charge the domesticated animals, very few of whom could withstand his shock. Beasts in this state therefore are occasionally killed by men with poisoned spears, who take up a position near their path and wound them as they pass; or by an arrow attached to a beam placed in their track, bent down and secured by a noose so arranged, that on its becoming disengaged by the action of an elephant's foot, the arrow flies up and strikes the animal's side.

All mines in Nepal are claimed as the property of the State, but I am induced to imagine, that the revenue derived from this source is decreasing, not from the store of mineral wealth throughout the country having been exhausted, for rich mines of iron, copper, arsenicate of copper, lead, sulphur and coal are still known to exist, moreover lumps of gold have been found in the beds of the hill streams, and several veins of silver are also stated to have been discovered; but the portion of the profits demanded by Government is so great, and, owing to the want of steam power and the mechanical appliances used in Europe, the expense of working mines is so heavy, that few speculators will come forward to undertake the contract; the lead mines which are the least profitable are in reality quite abandoned, and that ore is imported from British India.

The Gorkha miners do not in general sink a shaft from which the gallery diverges, but in the first instance run the gallery, or in some cases an open trench, from the surface at an angle of about 45 degrees, and when this is carried to such a depth that it fills with water, having no means of keeping it clear, the mine is deserted. Notwithstanding the disadvantages above described a large quantity of copper is still procured, and in the shape of rude paisa exported into the British territories, indeed to such an extent, that the districts of Gorukhpore, Champarun, Tirhoot and the parts of Oudh bordering on the Terai are deluged with these coins, and I question whether the whole of these Provinces absorb yearly 100 rupees in copper currency from the Calcutta Mint. The value of the Nepal paisa varies in every zillah, or in fact, I may say, in every village, but I should suppose the average rate would be about 22 gundas or 88 paisa per rupee.

In addition to the copper currency there is also a gold and silver coinage at the Nepal

Mint which yields some slight profits to the Government. Gold coins are called Ashrafis, and are subdivided into halves, quarters and eighths, but even these fractional parts are seldom used, and the full Ashrafi may be considered more in the light of a medal than a coin. The silver piece, in ordinary circulation, is styled a Mohur rupee and its value estimated at eight annas. Some few, named Siccas, are struck worth sixteen annas, but they are not common. The following table shows the relative value existing between the Nepal and Calcutta coinage.

The weight of Nepal Sicca Rupee	=	15¼ Calcutta annas.
Mohur or Adhidar................	=	7 annas and 7½ pice.
Quarter Mohur......................	=	1 anna and 10¼ pice.
Gold Rupee or Ashrafi...........	=	15 annas.

The standard of the silver coin is, 7 rupees 13 annas, and of the gold ditto, 2 rupees, per cent. less than the Calcutta Standard.

Various articles of export are subject to taxation, and an *ad valorem* duty of, 2½, per cent. is levied on all imports, from British India, moreover, besides other exactions in passing through the country with which I am unacquainted, but some of which are, I understand, vexatious, a charge of 4 annas per head, is made by the Durbar for every laden cooly passing the forts of Seesa Gurhee and Mukwanpore. I was, unfortunately, unable to obtain data sufficiently-precise to admit of my forming any calculation of the amount thus collected, but I was informed by an intelligent Sirdar, who for many years had charge of the Terai district, that he estimated the value of the goods annually exported to our territories, at nearly 12 lacs, and of those imported from the same quarter at about 9 lacs. Of the former, he enumerated the undermentioned articles:—Wax, ginger, timber of different sorts, pipal, (long pepper) pipla mul, (long pepper root) honey, hides, rushes, tez-pat, (Malabathrum leaf) stone, ivory, elephants, manjit, or the Indian madder, turmeric, nir bisi, (zedoary)

Jata masi, (spikenard) arsenic, orpiment, bezoar stone, kath, (Terra Japonica) musk, chilies, buffalo's horns, copper, oranges, walnuts, cardamums dèsce, Rāl or damar, resin, rice,* grain of different sorts,* charas, opium, ghee, lamp oil, bells, gongs, arms of different descriptions, and coarse paper; and amongst the latter, Lead, zinc, tin, pewter, soap, kapas, (raw cotton,) carpets, gold and silver lace, cotton goods of various descriptions, chintzes, muslins, &c., shawls, kinkabs, broadcloth, salt, dar chini, (cinnamon) supyari, (betel nut) pan, (betel leaf) sugar, black pepper, cloves, cardamums Guzratee, nutmegs, saffron, mace, saltpetre, sulphur, tobacco, alum, shells, mother-o'pearl, pearls, coral, beads, raw silk, sandal wood, shell lac, camphor, otters' skins,† glassware, plated glass and English cutlery. From China the importations are, Borax, furs, satins, silks, velvets, tea, rugs or

* From the Terai.

† From the neighbourhood of Dacca.

blankets, goats, dogs, ponies, preserved fruits, quicksilver, gold dust, yak-tail chaunries, chhattars, salamoniac, various medicinal drugs, and salt. The latter article is said to be brought from a lake about fifteen days' march beyond the Brahmaputra, and is transported on the backs of sheep, which owing to the length of the journey never return, but are sold at Kathmandhoo. These sheep are of a large size, and some of them have four horns, they carry a heavy load, the average weight being forty-two pounds.

The trade of Nepal is not at present extensive, but there is little doubt that under proper regulations, and with improved lines of communication, it might be so enlarged, as to become not only beneficial to its own Government and people, but also to those of the neighbouring States. It is not improbable, that together with their own exports, which consist principally of bells, cloths and arms, a few articles of British manufacture, even now, find their way to

Thibet through Kathmandhoo; but, as long as the roads in every direction, more especially those over the passes on the side of India, remain in their present wretched state, and the expense of carriage consequently continues so heavy, any increase of traffic in that quarter cannot reasonably be expected, and the inhabitants of that part of Asia, notwithstanding the spread of British power in the East, must, in a great measure, be dependant on Russia, both for the supply of goods of European workmanship, and as a mart for their own redundant productions. Whilst, in the event of commercial relations being once established on a firm footing between Hindustan and Thibet and Western China, taking into consideration the facility of water carriage for a great portion of the distance, and the shortness of the route as compared to that it now follows, it may with justice be inferred, that the whole of the trade connected with those countries, would speedily flow towards Calcutta.

Although the revenues of the Durbar may be, as compared to that of other States, trifling, yet as the Civil and Military functionaries, as already stated, are almost entirely remunerated by grants of land, and the Court is far from extravagant, the expenditure is also light, and there is consequently a considerable surplus annually realized, which would enable the Government to furnish funds for the general improvement of the means of communication throughout the country. Notwithstanding, to ensure the co-operation of the Sirdars, that it would be absolutely necessary, not only to impress them with a sense of the benefit which would accrue to their country from the extension of its commerce, but also to remove the fear, which they at present entertain, of an invasion by the British, in the event of the routes over the Seesa Gurhee and Mukwanpore passes being rendered easy of access, or new ones being opened; under the present, comparatively speaking, enlightened administration, and with the aid of European skill and science, there is reason to hope that eventually a new era may dawn upon Nepal, and she may become the great thoroughfare for circulating the traffic of Great Britain throughout the greater portion of the Celestial Empire. Having concluded this brief account of the Government of Nepal, I will now proceed, to the best of my power, to describe its inhabitants, their religion, habits, manufactures, &c.

CHAPTER III.

Inhabitants of Nepal—Estimated population—Distinct Tribes —Hindus—Muggurs—Gurungs—Kirats or Krats—Newars—Bhootias—Lepchas—Tharus—Religious toleration —Suttee—Court mourning—Diseases—Climate—Manufactures—Agriculture—Animal and Vegetable productions.

THE population of Nepal has never, I believe, been exactly ascertained, or at all events recorded; but from the accounts which have reached me, including the peasantry in the Terai and the inhabitants of the provinces bordering on the Brahmaputra, (who although perhaps hardly subject, are certainly tributary to the Gorkha Government,) I do not think I can be accused of exaggeration in estimating the number at not less than 4,000,000,* in which are comprised the undermentioned classes, differing both in language and habits, viz. pure Hindus, *i. e.* Brahmins and Khasiyas, (Hill Rajputs) Muggurs, Gurungs, Krats, Newars, Bhootias,

* I have heard it rated at over 5,000,000.

Lepchas and Tharus. My stay at Nepal was too short to enable me to enjoy an opportunity of making myself thoroughly acquainted with the customs peculiar to the various tribes, and I must therefore content myself with the following meagre sketch:—

The Hindus of the hills vary little, as regards the observance of religious ceremonies, from those of Hindustan; but, although equally strict in their intercourse with Europeans, amongst themselves they appear far less fettered by the prejudices of caste, and, with respect to partaking of animal food, pay much less attention to the precepts of Menu. In general, they eat readily of goats, sheep, (provided they are of the short-tailed breed) rabbits, ducks, duck's eggs, geese, turkeys, wild fowl, and game of all descriptions, (including the wild hog.) Many of them drink intoxicating liquors, prepared by fermentation from pines and other fruits. Like their brethren of the plains they worship the cow, but the unfortunate buffalo obtains little mercy at their hands, and the person who would not dare to aim the lightest blow at the former, does not hesitate, merely for the gratification of displaying his strength and skill, to deprive the latter of life; in fact, to cut off a buffalo's head with a single blow of the khora (a curved sword), is by no means a very uncommon feat amongst the Gorkhas.

The Muggurs appear to be one of the aboriginal races of Nepal; although they have adopted many of the customs of their Hindu conquerors, with the exception of abstaining from beef, they have no scruples as to their food, and are much addicted to intoxication.

The Gurungs are a pastoral tribe, whose manners assimilate in many respects to those of the Muggurs. They are worshippers of Budh and follow the doctrines of Sakya as explained by their own Lamas.*

* The Lamas are Budhist Monks, who have, nominally at least, forsaken the pleasures of the world. They reject

The Krats are a race formerly occupying the mountains to the East of Nepal Proper, where they still chiefly reside, they seem never to have become converts even to the liberal doctrines of the Hindus of the hills, but in a great measure to have preserved their own faith. They are not now permitted to kill kine, but I understand they always gladly avail themselves of every opportunity of regaling upon the flesh of a cow, which may have met with its death by accident.

The members of all the four classes above described are enlisted into the Gorkha army. They are generally bold, hardy, active and athletic men, and prove good soldiers.

the doctrine of caste, and admit a person of any nation into their order. They consider themselves under the authority of Sakya Gamba, who came from India about the beginning of our era, and resides at Lassa in perpetual youth, and is not therefore an Avatar. The Dherma Rajah, or spiritual Chief, of what we call Bhootan, is considered as an incarnation of a Boudh who has obtained divinity, and they believe that at the death of the body it inhabits, it passes into that of another child, and continues there through life, which is also believed of the Tishu Lama, the spiritual guide of the Chinese, who resides at Digarchi. The ordinary Lamas pretend only to be saints.

The Newars were the original holders of the valley of Nepal; although in the war with the Gorkhas they strove most gallantly to maintain their independence, they are now deemed too effeminate to be eligible for Military service, and are principally employed as traders, husbandmen and mechanics. In the latter capacity they are extremely skilful and expert, and, like the Chinese, will copy most minutely any pattern which may be given them, and if properly instructed, would make admirable artificers. At present they are the only carpenters and blacksmiths in Nepal, and many of the specimens of their workmanship are extremely well executed. They also excel as gold and silversmiths and their embroidery in pearls and other precious stones is well finished and in good taste.

They appear a quiet inoffensive race and are in general of a middle size, robust, with stout limbs and open and cheerful countenances; many of them have become proselytes to the Hindu religion, but the greater number are still followers of Budh; one sect denominated Bhamas shave their heads like the Bhootias and observe many of their religious rites as well as civil customs; they all burn their dead, and their principal characteristic is the little regard they entertain for the honor of their women, who are never confined or even kept under any restraint. When a girl is about eight years of age she is carried to a temple and married, with the ceremonies usual to Hindus, to the Bel fruit, (ægle marmelos) on her attaining the age of puberty, she is betrothed with her own consent to some man of the same caste, and receives a dower which becomes her husband's property; the nuptials are then celebrated with feasting and religious ceremonies; she is however at liberty to claim a divorce whenever she wishes, and on the slightest pretences; it is merely necessary before leaving the house, that she should signify her intention by placing two betel nuts in her bed, she is then free to choose another spouse; at the same time, provided she only cohabits with men of her own, or a higher caste, she can, whenever she pleases, return to the house of her first husband and resume charge of his family. Hamilton alludes to a custom which is still kept up amongst them. Sometime in May or June, a skirmish takes place between the young men and lads of the north and south ends of the town, which lasts 15 days, that on the fifteenth day is most serious, the opposing parties are drawn up in the broad, level, sandy bed of the river between the City and Sambhunath, the fight is carried on with stones—commences about an hour before sunset and continues until dark. Severe injuries are inflicted and occasionally a wound proves fatal. I have never heard the origin of the practice, but it is stated by the above mentioned author to be attributed to two causes, and the following is his account:—"Some allege, that at one time Kathmandhoo was subject to two Rajas and that the skirmishings first arose among their respective followers, and have ever since been continued; others, with more probability, think that the combat is meant to commemorate a battle between a son of Maha-Deva and a Rachhas or evil spirit. Colonel Crawfurd justly gives a preference to the latter opinion, for if one of the parties obtain the victory, every thing favorable, seasonable rains, plentiful crops, and fine weather is augured for the remainder of the year, the reverse is expected should the opposite party gain the advantage."

The Bhootias are of Tartar origin and inhabit the Provinces bordering on Thibet. They make their appearance at Kathmandhoo during the month of November, returning to their homes in March. They have two objects in visiting the Capital, to prosecute a lucrative traffic, and at the same time pay their adoration at the different Budhist shrines in the vicinity : they seem a cheerful and contented race, robust in person and filthy in their habits, I should conceive that a change of garments must be a luxury almost unknown amongst them. Their soil and climate being more favorable to animal than to vegetable life, they are chiefly restricted to the use of animal food, of which they generally obtain four meals per diem; they possess large herds of oxen, together with flocks of sheep and goats, and their country abounds in game of every description. Tea, they consume in large quantities, prepared with rancid lard, they also partake of spirituous liquors distilled principally from grain.

The Lepchas for the most part inhabit the country of Sikhim, but there are a few within the territories of the Nepal Government. From all accounts they are semi-barbarians, the use of fire-arms is little known amongst them, and they are principally armed with bows and arrows, they are very expert in handling their knives, which they employ either as weapons, or as tools in constructing huts, bridges, &c. I imagine they may be classed amongst the Budhists, as they have none of the scruples of Hindus with regard to their food.

The Tharus are the denizens of the Terai, and are said not to suffer from the deadly malaria, they are however sickly-looking men, and although from their being acclimatized, the poison may not work actively or rather speedily upon their frames, it is evident that their constitutions are debilitated and undermined from its effects, and their lives are, I believe, of short duration. To the eastward some districts of the Nepal dominions are inhabited by races, amongst others the Limbus, respecting whom I could acquire but little information, I have been however led to conjecture, that they are mere off-shoots from some of the tribes already specified.

Many of the domestic servants in Nepal are slaves; a male is styled Keta, and a female Ketee. I am not sufficiently acquainted with the subject to detail the circumstances under which the system of slavery is established, but I believe many slaves are born free, being the children of parties in necessitous circumstances and sold by their parents, others are hereditary slaves, being born in bondage, the progeny of persons who have lost their freedom; those attached to the households of men of rank, appear to be well treated, and are, in fact, on a superior footing in the family to hired menials.

Although the Gorkha Government would not in all probability allow its Hindu subjects to become converts either to Christianity or Mahomedanism, yet it is extremely tolerant as respects religion, and no one is subject to persecution on account of his faith. In the neighbourhood of Palpa there are, I understand, some Mussulman villages, the inhabitants of which were originally employed chiefly as Miners. Of their present pursuits, I have no exact knowledge.

Suttee is sanctioned throughout Nepal, but I am aware of several instances in which it has not been practised, and it is not considered dishonorable, on the part of the relatives, to dissuade a widow from being guilty of self-immolation, on the contrary, any person who may be convicted, of having used forcible or other unjustifiable means to induce a woman to sacrifice herself, is liable to severe punishment. The argument which I have heard advanced against the prohibition of the practice, was, the futility of attempting to suppress it with a view to prevent the loss of life, as in the event of a woman being determined, either from affection to the deceased, or as a point of honor, to accompany her husband's corpse to the grave, or rather funeral pile, she would commit suicide by taking poison, or by other means which could not possibly be guarded against.

On the occasion of the demise of a member of the Royal Family general mourning is strictly enforced. Every person is prohibited for the period of one year from attending any place of festivity, listening to the sounds of music, and wearing shoes in which a single particle of leather is introduced. For three days nobody can enter a carriage, eat more than once a day, or partake of food prepared with spices, moreover, it is incumbent on every one to shave the head and wear the (Tilak Matam dari ki) mark of grief or mourning, on the forehead.

The diseases prevalent in Nepal are fever, rheumatism, goitre, cutaneous disorders and venereal; the latter is particularly common, for all classes are most dissolute. The Natives of the plains when residing in the valley of Kathmandhoo, are, equally with the inhabitants, subject to Bronchocele. The residents of some localities are however exempt from this malady, amongst others, those living in the villages of Kirtapur and

Sanchu, both of which are situated on eminences: cases of leprosy or elephantiasis seldom, if ever, occur amongst the Nepalese.

The climate of Nepal is superior to that of Hindustan, and, as the temperature is several degrees cooler, I should suppose better suited to the European constitution. During the few days of my stay at Kathmandhoo, early in February, the Thermometer in an open room never rose above 65°. The Gorkhas divide their year into six seasons, but this is, I presume, an error, as they almost exactly correspond with those of the plains. The rains commence a little earlier, and set in from the south-east quarter; they are usually very copious and break up towards the middle of October. The torrents from the mountains being often extremely violent at this period, while the descent of the rivers through the low lands is not sufficiently precipitate, as to carry off the waters with rapidity; they are very liable to overflow their banks, and thus during the months of July, August and September, two-thirds of the valley is generally inundated. Throughout the cold season, *i. e.* from October to March, dense fogs are extremely prevalent; they however generally clear off about 9 or 10 A. M. when they are succeeded by bright sunshine, but the solar rays have but little power, and it is quite possible to be exposed to them the whole day without suffering from their influence. The principal manufactures of Nepal are arms, chain armour, brass utensils and ornaments, bells, of which they export a large number to India, one or two sorts of coarse, and one fine cotton cloth, the latter, called Maleeda, is particularly soft and light, and a coarse kind of paper, which is prepared in enormous sheets in the following manner:—The pulp, made from the bark of a shrub, of which it is composed, is spread upon a sheet tightly stretched on a frame extended over a small tank, containing sufficient water to cover it; when it is completely saturated, the water is drained off, and the paper dried by artificial heat, produced by pans of burning charcoal placed under the frame.

The tree of which the bark is used for the above purpose is the Sied burrooa, a Species of Daphne. There are two kinds, both growing to a considerable size, the one is called Kaghazi pat, or the paper plant, and the other the Bhootia Sied burrooa, or paper tree of Thibet, which is deemed the best.

The valley of Nepal is extremely fertile, in many places yielding no less than 4 crops per annum, viz. wheat, rice, Indian corn, (maki) and vegetables. Owing to the prejudices of the Hindu with respect to the treatment of the ox, and the want of any other description of draught cattle, the plough is seldom, if ever, seen, and the soil is prepared by hand, the implement used being a kind of hoe. Although this system of husbandry must necessarily entail a greater amount of labor, it is in other respects equally efficacious as the method adopted in Hindustan; in fact, were the plough alone to be used in Nepal, many plots of land which are now under cultivation, would be abandoned, as, consequent on the inequality of the surface of the country, the fields have for the most part to be formed in a succession of small terraces along the sides of the numerous hills. The soil is in general rich, consisting of a mixture of light mould, sand and gravel, supported by a deep black unctuous earth, which latter, the cultivators spread over the rice fields as manure.

The operations of husbandry are of course tedious, and at some seasons, every person, in the family capable of labor, must be employed, consequently no one being available to remain in charge of the young children, they are taken to the field, and the villager may be seen carrying his infants in two baskets suspended over his shoulder by a bamboo. Towards the end of the rainy season shooting is strictly prohibited, not from any desire to preserve the game, but in order that the services of the sportsmen may be at liberty to aid in getting in the harvest.

Land in Nepal is divided into khets or fields, each of which is estimated to produce a certain number of bushels of paddy or rice in the husk, the subdivisions are as follows:

20 Pathils = 1 Muri.
20 Muris = 1 Biswa.
5 Biswas = 1 Khet.

Although the country is everywhere intersected with streams, which might be made available for the purpose of irrigation, and the people are perfectly well aware of their great value in this respect, yet from not possessing the means of conducting the water to the high grounds, a large portion is entirely wasted, and land which might otherwise afford a profitable return to the cultivator remains untilled; the water-power at their command is however employed by the Gorkhas to work their numerous mills for grinding corn.

My attainments as a Zoologist and Botanist do not, I regret to confess, admit of my preparing a scientific report, and I must be therefore satisfied with submitting a very concise account of the animal and vegetable productions of Nepal. The description of sheep most common is a small kind, called the Barwal, it affords when properly fed, very fair mutton. Oxen are not numerous, as milch cows alone can be prized for their useful qualities, little trouble probably is taken in their breeding, the milk of the latter is however said to be extremely rich; buffaloes are generally brought up from the plains. I was informed that horses are bred at Peutana, but only one specimen came under my observation, he was a sturdy cob about 14¼ hands high. Ponies are numerous, but few are, I imagine, indigenous, being chiefly imported from Thibet. The dog, generally known as the Nepal dog, is also properly speaking a native of Thibet, it is a fierce surly creature, about the size of an English bull dog and covered with thick long hair; there are several other classes of the canine species, but it is out of my power to describe them, nor are they hardly deserving of notice. Elephants, rhinoceroses, tigers, leopards, bears, hogs, jackals, foxes, antelopes, musk, hog, and spotted deer, and many individuals of the monkey race, are to be found in the thick jungle which skirts the hills to the south-west, and wild horses and sheep are occasionally seen on the range of mountains to the north.

Of the feathered tribes the most remarkable are the falcon used by sportsmen, the hill maina, and the monal and damphia, of the pheasant genus, the former being of the spotted and the latter of the golden species, the chikor, florican, black and grey partridge, woodcock, snipe, quail, teal and wild duck are also procurable, but many of them only appear as birds of passage, making Nepal their resting place, in their migration from Hindustan to Thibet.

Nepal would doubtless afford a fine field for the researches of the botanist. The forests of the Terai contain the sal, siso, semal, mimosa, (from which catechu is extracted) ebony and other trees; in the higher regions, oaks, chesnuts, hollies, yews, laurels and pines are abundant; the principal fruit trees are the mulberry, raspberry, orange, apples, kaphul, (apparently a sort of cherry,) and walnut, together with some kinds of plum, pears and peaches are also numerous, but the fruit seldom ripens. There are, I believe, many species of the rhododendron (gurus), orchideous plants of various descriptions seem to abound, and specimens of the Victoria Regia are also said to have been discovered in the woods.

The only herbs of any pretensions, which I have heard mentioned, are the charita, which is extremely bitter and much used in India for febrile diseases, the zedoary (curcuma zedoaria) a spicy plant somewhat like ginger in its leaves, and of a sweet scent, the jatamasi (spikenard) and khet bish, the root of which is said to be a violent poison.

Lettuces, spinach, French beans, garlic, radishes and numerous other vegetables are cultivated in the valley of Kathmandhoo. Potatoes do not flourish in Nepal Proper, but are brought in great quantities from the Juxta Himalayan tracts.

Fish are found in abundance in the rivers of the Terai, mullet and a species of carp being the most common.

CHAPTER IV.

Boundaries of Nepal—Rivers—Lakes—City of Kathmandhoo—Situation—Streets—Temples—Population—City of Patan—Newar remains—Bhatgaon—Kirtapur, &c.

THE Kingdom of Nepal consists of a succession of mountain ranges and valleys situated between India and Thibet, and running for about 400 miles parallel to the north-east frontier of the British territories; it formerly extended in a westerly direction almost to Cashmere, but is now circumscribed within the left bank of the Kalee Nuddee, the whole of their possessions beyond that stream having been wrested from the Gorkhas in the war of 1815. To the eastward, the State of Sikhim (where we have a Military post,) forms the boundary, thus, on three sides it is in immediate contact with our power and accessible to our arms. The north-eastern frontier of the dominions of the sovereigns of Nepal, does not appear to be very clearly defined, but although it is probable that the Rajah exercises little power over some of the tribes dwelling beyond the Alpine region of the Himalayas, on the banks of the Brahmaputra, yet, as I have before mentioned, they acknowledge themselves as tributaries, and consequently that river may be deemed the boundary.

The mountain ridges of Nepal are everywhere intersected by streams of various sizes, all of which, after winding through the fertile plains of India, eventually disembogue their waters into the bed of the Ganges. The principal of these are the Gogra, Gunduk, Raptee and Kousie, which chiefly serve to float down to Calcutta, the valuable timber abounding in the forests by which the lower ranges of hills are skirted. Four lakes of considerable magnitude are said to exist in the direction of Gorkha, one of which is called the Burwal and another the Gurhwal Tal, but the accounts which I have heard regarding them, vary to so great an extent, as to preclude my entering into any description either as to their size or locality.

As, in treating of the country of Nepal, it may not be amiss to describe its capital. I shall now offer a few remarks with respect to Kathmandhoo.

The city of Kathmandhoo is situated within a valley, running from north to south about 16, and from east to west 12 miles, its form is oval, and circuit between 40 and 50 miles, its altitude is estimated at 4,700 feet; it is watered by the Bag Mati and Bish Mati rivers, and on all sides bounded by ranges of mountains; sinking towards the westward, but in other places rising to a great height, beyond which, however, on a clear day, the lofty peaks of the Dewal Geree, Jibjibbeah, Gosain Than, and other points in the snowy range are plainly discernible.

The most remarkable mountains in the lower range are Sewaporee to the north, Debee Kot on the east, and Chundra Geree on the south-west. Snow frequently lies for days on the summits of these heights, and the slope on the north side of the first-mentioned was thickly covered in the beginning of February 1851. Although the area of the valley is considerable, in no part is a plain of any extent to be found, as, from the ranges of hills by which it is surrounded, spurs project in every direction, many of which are gradually prolonged to a great distance, breaking up the face of the country into a series of undulations, everywhere intersected by hill streams, of which the most important are the two mentioned in the preceding paragraph. On the east bank of one of which, the Bish Mati, the City of Kathmandhoo is situated, following its course for about a mile until its junction with the Bag Mati; this latter is crossed by two bridges of masonry, one leading from the Tundee Khel parade ground towards Lalita Patan, and the other from the Palace to the principal Magazine. Both these rivers are broad shallow streams, and in the cold season at all points passable by foot passengers, for whose accommodation, however, temporary bridges, composed of a succession of single planks resting on upright beams as supports, are in many places established.

The town is little superior to the generality of Native Cities, the streets are narrow, rudely paved, and for the most part extremely dirty, the houses in general of brick, two and three stories in height, with curiously carved wooden balconies and lattices; the Palace is a straggling building of no pretensions, near it, forming a sort of square, are several temples, differing however from those in India, and far more resembling Chinese pagodas; they are ornamented on the outside by wooden figures most grotesquely carved and painted, one of them is entirely constructed of wood (Kath), hence, I was informed, the origin of the name given to the City; in the neighbourhood of this open space are the two principal Courts, the Eta Chaplee and the Kothee Ling. I also observed a temple dedicated to Bheem Sen, the son of Pandu, a favorite deity of the Gorkhas. In front of this building is a column surmounted by a brazen winged-lion, having near it a pedestal, on which a statue, representing a kneeling celestial-figure, (Gurur) is placed.

There are one or two market places, which appeared crowded with men of all castes and tribes, from the natives of the burning plains of India to the uncivilized Bhootias from the snow-capped hills of Thibet. The buildings in the vicinity of the city most deserving of attention are the temples of Pasupati Nath, Sambhu Nath, Balajee and Budh.

The shrine of Pasupati Nath, dedicated to Siva, is built upon the edge of the Bag Mati, which is there considered a holy stream, and consequently every true Hindu is desirous of yielding up his last breath on its sacred banks: the spot assigned for the cremation of members of the Royal Family, is between two small bridges adjoining the building. This temple is esteemed the holiest in Nepal, and is of such sanctity that pilgrims from India visit it, and consider the pilgrimage one of great devotion; it consists of several squares containing shrines consecrated at different periods. The principal sanctuary is in the shape of a pagoda having a leaden roof, the ridges of which are covered with a substance resembling copper gilt; our Ciceroni informed us that it was a thin sheet of gold, but I take the liberty of doubting his accuracy on this head; the walls immediately under the eaves, were adorned with a very extraordinary description of ornament, viz., the

*

various offerings that have been made to the deity, and the arms, culinary utensils, &c. of persons dying (La Waris) without heirs, and, as may be imagined, a most strange assemblage of articles; swords, shields, pots, pans, looking-glasses, buffalo horns, knives, bracelets and spinning wheels, were to be seen suspended by hooks and nails, from every point. In the centre of the building, I observed two massive silver doors, supported on either side by curiously carved wood work. Within the court-yard, where, by the bye, Europeans are not admitted, is the figure of Nanda, the sacred bull, also several representations of Hindu deities; the outer gates are flanked by sculptured lions. Opposite to the temple is the sacred jungle, appropriated apparently to the sole use of the monkeys that infest it.

The temple of Sambhu Nath is a Budhist shrine in honor of Maha Deva, only resorted to by the Bhootias and Bhamas (a tribe of Newars,) and considered the most ancient edifice in Nepal. Hamilton supposes that its erection may have taken place about the beginning of the 8th century; it is situated on a well-wooded eminence to the west of the Bish Mati, and is the most conspicuous building throughout the valley; the path by which it is approached, ascending to the summit of the hill by a flight of about 200 steep stone steps. The centre edifice is quadrangular, surmounted by a dome and high spire, covered with plates of copper gilt; on the four sides, are recesses protected by iron lattice work, three of these niches being occupied by large brazen images, and the fourth, fronting the entrance to the court, by two similar figures on a smaller scale. There are other buildings around it, but they hardly need description; from one point near the temple there is a lovely view of the city and valley.

The temple of Balajee is about two miles from Kathmandhoo, in a north-easterly direction. It is only remarkable for its tanks, in one of which, is a representation, in stone, of Siva resting on a bed of snakes, another is filled with tame fish, which, in the hope of being fed, approach the by-stander without fear.

The temple of Budh is a strange earthen cupola surmounted by a spire, upon which, in the brightest of colors, is delineated a face with staring eyes; it is placed within a court-yard surrounded by buildings inhabited by Bhootias during their periodical visits to Nepal.

In addition to these buildings there is near the Tundee Khel Parade ground, a fine column, nearly 200 feet in height, built, I understand, by Bheem Sing, when Minister.

The population of Kathmandhoo may be rated at 40,000, but within the limits of the valley there must be about 400,000 persons, as it contains several large towns and villages, amongst them Patan, Bhatgaon, Pheer Phing, Kirtapur and Than Kot.

The City next in importance to Kathmandhoo is the ancient capital, Patan, situated on a rising ground to the south-east and about two miles distant. During the Newar dynasty it was the residence of Royalty, but when the tide of invasion setting in from Gorkha, swept away no less than 24 independent principalities, it became involved in the general ruin, and the seat of Government was transferred by the conquerors to its present locality. From that date the decay of Patan commenced. It is still, however, a considerable town, abounds in fine buildings, and is consequently well worthy a visit; at one extremity, opposite the ruins of the Palace of the former Kings, are several temples, near which, on two carved monoliths, are brazen statues, the one, a Monarch, in a sitting posture, with a cobra, on which a bird is perched, rearing its head behind him,* the other similar to that, already described, near

* An incident similar to that apparently represented by the above group, occurred in the life of Rajah Sanga, of Cheetore, who, when in exile, was, owing to thi[illegible]
by a goatherd. The bird of omen is [illegible]

*

Bheem Sen's temple at Kathmandhoo. I noticed here several sculptured figures of maned lions, much resembling those discovered at Nineveh, two on each side of the flight of steps leading to every temple, the two hinder ones being invariably represented with beaks like birds. Some of the temples were of the pagoda style of architecture, but most of them consisted of conically shaped domes rising out of clusters of small shrines, the latter being generally erected on a rectangular base about 12 feet in height.

Bhatgaon is about eight miles from Kathmandhoo, it is said to boast of some fine buildings.

Kirtapur is situated on a rising ground about 3 miles west from Patan. Here a most desperate defence was made by the Newars, and it was consequently almost the last place subdued by the Gorkhas, who, in revenge for the loss they experienced before it, upon its being taken, barbarously mutilated all the male inhabitants, cutting off their lips and noses, and changed the name of the town to Naskatapur, which signifies the city of cut noses. It contains a large temple, adorned in a similar manner to the shrine at Pasupati Nath. Sculptured lions are also seen mixed with figures of elephants on the steps leading to some of the sacred buildings. Pheer Phing I have alluded to in a previous Chapter. Than Kot is a thriving hamlet near the foot of the Chundra Geree pass, and about seven miles from Kathmandhoo.

My limited sojourn in Nepal precluded my gaining information on many points which might have proved interesting either to the politician, antiquarian, or scientific reader, I must therefore fain be content, with having made even this slight addition to our stock of knowledge regarding this remote country, and shall now proceed to narrate some of the events most worthy of note that have occurred within the kingdom during the last few years.

CHAPTER V.

History of Nepal—Establishment of the Gorkha Rule—Conquests of Prithi Narain—Reigns of Singha Pratap and Rana Bahadur Sah—Nepalese incursion into Thibet—Repulse by Tartar Troops and subsequent invasion of Nepal—British Embassy—Outrageous conduct of Rana Bahadur—His abdication and return to power—Second British Mission—Assassination of Rana Bahadur—Accession to the throne of Rajah Girivan Juddhu Bickram Sah—Encroachments of the Gorkhas on the British Territories—Negotiations—Murder of the Thannadar of Chilwah—Nepal War—Destruction of the British Detachments at Pursa and Summundpore—Repulse of General Wood's Division—Failure of the attack on Kalunga—Investment of Jyetuk—Operations under General Ochterlony—Terms of capitulation granted to Ummur Sing—Occupation of the Province of Kemaon—Negotiations renewed—Advance of the force under General Ochterlony—Treaty of peace ratified by the Durbar.

Although this narrative was originally intended to be confined merely to events which have taken place within the last ten years, I have deemed it necessary, as a preliminary to the recital of the scenes of intrigue and bloodshed which must be therein depicted, to offer a few observations relative to the previous history of the Royal Family and the administration of Government under their rule, together with a short account of the circumstances which led to the rupture with the British in 1814, and the subsequent Military operations.

The Rajah of Nepal assumes descent from the Rajput Princes of Oudeepore,* and I have been assured that papers are still in the possession of the Durbar which would fully substantiate this pretension, yet the point has certainly never been proved, and I question whether his claim to be styled a member of that family would be acknowledged by the present Rana. It is asserted, that on leaving the plains of India, the Rajah's ancestry settled in the vicinity of Palpa, but gradually made encroachments on the neighbouring territories until they obtained

* It is stated by Col. Tod that the Gorkha Dynasty was founded, towards the end of the 12th century, by the third son of Rajah Samarsi, ruler of Cheetore.

*

dominion over the city and province of Gorkha, from which their name was derived. Here they established their rule, and remained for several generations without displaying any wish to extend their power. About the middle of the last century, however, Prithi Narain succeeded his father, Ner Bhopal Sah, and being a man of great ambition, with little scruple as to the equity of the measures he might take in order to indulge his desires, seized the opportunity of an application for succour from the Ruler of Bhatgaon, then waging war with the other kings of Nepal, to take advantage of their dissensions, and commenced a series of aggressive movements towards the eastward, which, after a protracted warfare, finally terminated in the conquest of the valley of Nepal, and the entire overthrow of the different petty states in that quarter. To the British historian, these operations offer some little interest, owing to the discomfiture of the detachment under Captain Kinloch in 1765, dispatched, it is said, by the Indian Government, to the aid of the last of the Suruj Bansi Dynasty who reigned over Kathmandhoo, when attacked by his treacherous ally, or rather feudatory; this force penetrated as far as Hureehurpur, but was not strong enough to maintain its communications with the plains, and, having advanced into the hills at least a month too soon (October), its progress was arrested by an unfordable nullah, across which a bridge was constructed but speedily carried away by the force of the torrent. The delay thus experienced exhausted the supplies, disease became prevalent, and it was obliged to effect a retreat early in December.

A graphic account of the campaign in 1768, when Prithi Narain made himself master of Kathmandhoo, is given by father Guiseppe, a member of the Catholic Mission which had been long established in Nepal, where they had secured many converts and received grants of land from the Newar monarchs, the title deeds of which, inscribed on copper, are still in the possession of the Bishop of Patna. Permission was granted to the Christians to retire into the British territories, of which most of the proselytes availed themselves and settled at Bettiah, some emigrated to Lassa and Diggurcha, where their descendants still reside, and a few apparently remained in Nepal, as the church was in existence in 1802, on the arrival of Captain Knox's mission. The Reverend father describes the cruelties inflicted on the inhabitants of the captured towns as being almost beyond imagination; at one time, fearing to succeed in reducing the inhabitants of the valley to subjection, by the sword; the Gorkha King determined to effect his purpose by famine, and with this design, stationed troops at all the passes of the mountains to prevent any intercourse with Nepal. His orders were most rigorously obeyed, for every person who was found on the road, with merely a little salt or cotton about him, was hung upon a tree, and he caused all the inhabitants of one village to be put to death in the most cruel manner, neither men, women, nor children, being allowed to escape, for having supplied a small quantity of the latter article to the Nepalese.

The demise of Prithi Narain occurred, according to Kirkpatrick, in 1771, and his successor Singha Pratap, who reigned only 3 years, seems to have fully adopted his father's course of policy, and annexed to his dominions several districts to the south-west. At his death the sovereignty descended upon his infant son, Rana Bahadur Sah, who was on the throne in 1793, when the first British mission entered Nepal. He appears, even when of an age to have taken a part in the conduct of affairs, to have been for some time completely guided by the Regents, in the first instance, the Ranee Rajundra Luchmi, and subsequently his uncle Bahadur Sah, both of whom were actuated by a love of conquest, and added numerous provinces to the territories of the house of Gorkha, which were now advanced beyond Kemaon. In 1792, the misunderstanding took place between the Durbar and the Imperial Court, and the advance of the victorious Tartar army deprived the former of all hope of future conquest; they were even so far terrified as to seek the aid of the British. The Governor General, Lord Cornwallis, whilst he distinctly refused compliance with their application for a Military force, agreed to mediate between the contending powers, and his offer having been accepted by the Durbar, in February 1793, Col. Kirkpatrick was deputed on a Mission to Kathmandhoo. Ere however he reached the Frontier, peace had been re-established, and consequently, all occasion for the good offices of the British having ceased, although every courtesy was shown to the party; little cordiality was evinced in their reception, and a commercial treaty having been previously concluded by a Native agent, no object existed for prolonging their stay, and they soon retraced their steps. The origin of hostilities with the Emperor appears to have been as follows:—About 1780, Samhur Lama having fled from Lassa to Nepal, taking with him a considerable quantity of treasure, the Rajah reeeived him under his protection and bestowed upon him a jagir. Subsequently, the Lama, by accounts of the Chinese Empire, and of the gold, silver and other mines in the neighbourhood of Lassa, excited the avarice and eupidity of the Government, and an expedition was formed which crossing the frontier entered Bhoat (Thibet) and was vietorious in several engagements with the Bhootia troops. The Officer commanding the latter, finding himself unable to resist the invaders, was forced to succumb, and a treaty was concluded, under the provisions of which, not only was a tribute of three lacs of rupees settled on the Rajah of Nepal; but it was determined that all coin at the Lassa Mint should be stamped in his name. In consequence of the superiority which had prevailed in favor of the Nepal troops over those of Lassa throughout this campaign, in 1785, during the administration, as Governor General, of Sir John Macpherson, the rulers of the latter State sent a deputation to Calcutta demanding assistance, which, however, was not accorded.

In 1789-90, Samhur Lama having again worked upon the avaricious disposition of the Durbar, induced them to dispatch a force of 18,000 men to Diggurcha (Teeshoo Lumboo), where they plundered the treasury, and seized a Vazir of Lassa, deputed to enter into a negotiation for peace. On their return, encumbered with the spoils of the city, although the winter was considerably advanced, they were induced to take the Khartah and Hutterah route instead of the ordinary one by Koot, and were consequently exposed to great perils in crossing the ridge of mountains, which stretches in a north-east direction from the vicinity of Koot, to the country of the Limbus and of the Deva Durma; it was with the utmost difficulty and danger that they penetrated through the snow with which their tract was covered, to a depth that proved fatal, in several instances, on the slightest false step. They were in this dreadful situation for five or six days, during which, they were obliged to pass the night on the pure snow, which they hardened to the best of their power, though their labor was sometimes scarcely completed, ere a fresh fall would almost bury them. The loss of the army in this retreat, which was conducted by Damodar Pandee and Bum Sah, is said to have amounted to upwards of 2,000 men, the greater number of whom appear to have been frozen to death; many deemed themselves happy in escaping, with the loss of their fingers and toes.

The Emperor of China, hearing of this proceeding, sent a wakil to Kathmandhoo, to protest against the unjustifiable aggression and demand redress; he was, however, received most cavalierly, and returned without succeeding in the object of his Mission. On his arriving in China, and stating the result of his embassy, the Emperor's indignation was aroused at the insolence of the Durbar, and a force consisting of 70,000 men was directed to march on Nepal, under the orders of an Imperial Officer styled Sund Fo. The Rajah was called upon to surrender Samhur Lama, the instigator of the disputes, and also the Vazir who had been taken prisoner; but he refused to give up the former. Sund Fo accordingly formed his army into two divisions, one of 30,000 and the other of 40,000 men, and passing to the eastward under the hills to Trisul Gunga, penetrated beyond Khan Rowan. Here he intercepted a large body of Gorkhas returning from the army, which, under

Damodar Pandee, had attacked and taken Chunga,—a desperate battle ensued; but the Nepalese troops having been hemmed in between the two divisions, were completely defeated, and their leader Perpiera Thakur wounded. The Tartar army continued its march, and after successively repulsing the different Gorkha detachments which opposed its progress, reached Nyakot early in September 1792, when the Durbar, as already stated, were forced to sue for peace, which was granted, although on humiliating terms. The Lama had previously, to prevent being delivered into the hands of the Chinese General, poisoned himself.

For sometime the Gorkhas were fully employed in consolidating their power within the limits of their recently-acquired possessions; the Court also became the scene of intrigue, and in 1795, the Regent having been removed from office, died in confinement.

On assuming the reins of Government, Rana Bahadur gave full vent to his ungovernable passions, and neglecting his wife, the daughter of the Gulmi Rajah, he openly cohabited with other women. First, he had a son by a common slave, and afterwards another, by the daughter of a Brahman. This gave great offence to the Priests, who, as a means of disturbing him, published a prophecy, foretelling that the Rajah would not long survive his beautiful favorite of the sacred order, she was soon after attacked with smallpox, and having suffered much from the ravages of the disease, on her recovery, out of grief at the loss of her beauty, poisoned herself; Rana Bahadur, having great faith in the science of astrology, had been in the utmost consternation during her sickness, and, at the instigation of the astrologers, had advanced a large sum for the performance of certain ceremonies before one of the gods. He now wreaked his vengeance upon the Brahmans, whom he scourged, in order to make them disgorge the money; and destroying the image, ground it to pieces, causing the fragments to be thrown into the river. Many of the other deities shared the same fate; guns being even opened upon them, to complete the work of destruction; the people, terrified at his violence, and horror-struck at his impiety, became ripe for a change, and, at last, in 1800, to prevent the necessity of his being deposed, or put to death, it was suggested, that he should resign in favor of his son and retire to Benares. Although with reluctance, he followed the advice thus tendered, and, for some time, under the plea of insanity, resided at the holy city; whilst there, he incurred a considerable debt to the British Government, in consequence of which, a treaty was entered into, providing for the residence of a British officer at Kathmandhoo. The Mission entered the Gorkha territories in February 1802, and not meeting with a very favorable reception, left Nepal, on its return to India, in March 1803. Soon after, Rana Bahadur quitted Benares and proceeded to Kathmandhoo, where he resumed his former power, and with it, the old Gorkha policy, which, in fact, can never be said to have been quite lost sight of, as in 1798, an attack had been made upon the territories of the Rajah of Sikhim. It, in the first instance, proved unsuccessful, but ultimately, the Durbar succeeded in wresting from him a portion of his territories. Ummur Sing Thapa was now dispatched with a large army to the westward, and seizing Gurhwal and the country beyond the Jumna, rapidly extended the Gorkha power, which would have spread to Cashmere, had he not, in 1810, been foiled before Kot Kangra, principally, owing to the superior address of the old Lion of the Punjab, Runjeet Sing.

Rana Bahadur did not long enjoy his sovereignty, for having by his tyranny exasperated many of the principal Chiefs, the feeling of hostility to his rule again became general, and in 1805, upon his issuing an order to his brother Shere Bahadur to join the army in the field, the latter refused to obey, an altercation ensued, when he drew his sword, and, in open Durbar, inflicted upon the Rajah a wound, which proved mortal, being himself almost instantaneously killed by Bheem Sing Thapa, a Sirdar who was present on the occasion, and who subsequently became vested with the entire management of the State.

For a considerable period Bheem Sing, as Regent, ruled over Nepal with uncontrolled and undisputed authority, Rajah, Maha Rajah, Girivan Juddha Bikram Sah, the illegitimate son of the deceased, whose life was saved by his being secreted in the women's apartments during the affray which ensued upon his father's murder, and who now succeeded to the throne, being a mere infant, whilst the greater number of the Sirdars who might have interfered in the administration of affairs, had been removed by the Thapa, who took advantage of the Rajah's assassination to accomplish the massacre of every Chief, whose influence he dreaded; under the plea of his having been concerned in the conspiracy, which, certainly, in most cases, is supposed not to have been quite devoid of foundation, although their guilt may not have been fully established. It is stated that about three hundred persons perished on this occasion.

In consequence of the want of cordiality evinced by the Durbar, the treaty of amity concluded by Captain Knox was declared dissolved by the Governor General in Council, in 1804, and a letter, stating the grounds on which the resolution was founded, transmitted to the Rajah on the 24th January of that year; a semblance of friendship was, however, still maintained between the two States.

Encroachments on the part of the Nepalese took place in the district of Tirhoot as far back as 1787, and were stigmatized by the Marquis of Hastings, as having been marked by features of violence in their origin, and of evasion and duplicity when they became a subject of investigation. These aggressions were brought to the notice of Government in 1798; but, owing, most probably, to the necessity for employing all our resources towards the overthrow of the French power in the Deccan, and the prosecution of the campaign against Tippoo Sultan; whilst, at the same time, it was requisite to hold a force in readiness on the North West frontier to resist the threatened invasion of Zaman Shah; no decisive steps were taken for the expulsion of the intruders, although in the first instance a representation was addressed to the Rajah. Subsequently, in 1804, instructions were issued to the Magistrate to institute enquiries on the subject; but, notwithstanding the utter defeat of the Mahratta confederacy, by which, towards the close of 1805, the British troops were left at full liberty to turn the whole weight of their arms against the

Gorkhas; no further notice seems to have been taken of their unjustifiable conduct.

This moderation on the part of the Indian Government, as, has been always the case in our intercourse with Native States, was doubtless attributed to our weakness, and a disinclination to an encounter with the hardy mountaineers, who prided themselves upon their superiority over the enervated inhabitants of the plains, and were, moreover, naturally a good deal inflated with the almost unvaried success which they had experienced in their operations to the westward. Thus emboldened, the encroachments of the Gorkhas became more frequent; restitution was occasionally demanded, and investigations were ordered, but the Nepalese Officers employed upon them, invariably avoided bringing their proceedings to a close, and even, by menaces, compelled the native officials in the British service to retire from the disputed territories, which they continued to occupy.

Affairs upon the frontier remained in this unsatisfactory state until 1812, up to which period, it was calculated that nearly two hundred villages had been usurped by the Nepalese.

In May 1813, Ummur Sing Thapa, the Gorkha Commander beyond the Jumna, who had previously, in December 1809, been apprised by General Ochterlony, that although, as long as the operations of his troops were confined to the hilly country, no interference would be offered by the British, he must distinctly understand, that he would not be permitted to violate the territories in the plains, chiefly belonging to the Seikh States under our protection, advanced claims to four villages at the foot of the hills, on the groundless pretext of their forming a part of the district of Batowlee, of which the rest was situated within the mountains, and had fallen under the dominion of the Durbar. These villages were invested and seized by the Gorkha troops.

The General immediately remonstrated against the measure, and declared, that unless they at once evacuated the lands, the Government would resort to arms to compel them. This threat proved effectual, and the Gorkhas reluctantly abandoned the villages, to which they had not the shadow of a right.

I have already alluded to the evasions practised by the Nepalese officers, to prevent the acknowledgment of the just rights of the British, whenever investigations were held relative to the unwarrantable aggressions of the Gorkhas. For several years, a correspondence had been carried on respecting the claim of the former to the districts of Bootwal (with the exception of the town) and Sheoraj; although the right of the British to both was incontestable, the Durbar were informed, that, on the condition of the immediate relinquishment of the first named, the second would be forthwith transferred to them. To this equitable and liberal proposition no reply was vouchsafed. In

1809, a letter was addressed to the Rajah, calling on him to withdraw his troops from the disputed territory; his answer was vague and unsatisfactory, a desire was, however, expressed, that the matter might be adjusted by a commission composed of officers appointed by both Governments. Soon after further encroachments were made,* and in an affray which took place with the tenants of the Rajah of Bettiah, perfectly unprovoked on their part, a Nepalese Subah Lachmi Ger and several others, on both sides, were slain.

It was now signified to the Nepal wakil that the Government was determined, if necessary, to resist the recent usurpations by force, but would, nevertheless, being anxious that the question should be decided amicably, accept the Rajah's offer.

* It is stated as an instance of the insolence of the Gorkhas that a Fakir appeared at the burial place of some Mahomedan Saints, within the limits of the Honourable Company's territory, with a grant from the Rajah of Nepal of the offerings made at the shrines.

Colonel Bradshaw was accordingly appointed Commissioner on the part of the British, and proceeded to Gorukhpore and afterwards to Bootwul, where he was met by the Nepalese officers and commenced to carry out the orders with which he had been furnished.

The validity of the claims of the British were fully established, yet their justice would not be admitted by the Nepalese Commissioners, who proposed a compromise; the Governor General, Lord Minto, however, deeming the proof that had been adduced, irrefragable, refused to relinquish any part of the territorial possessions of the Honourable Company. The Marquis of Hastings now assumed the reins of Government, and finding that the Nepalese still endeavoured to evade recognizing the just rights of the British, determined to assert those rights by force, and Colonel Bradshaw was accordingly instructed to demand, either from the Durbar, or Commissioners, a formal renunciation of their pretensions to certain villages at Nunnore and of the surrender of the lands on the Sarun frontier still in their possession, at the same time, he was directed to intimate explicitly, but in a temperate manner, that, unless this demand should be complied with, the necessary measures would be adopted for enforcing the claim.

On the receipt of these instructions, the Colonel addressed a note to the Nepalese Commissioners, proposing a meeting for the purpose of discussing the former proceedings; in reply, they declined holding any further communication with him, and directed him to quit the frontier, soon after they returned to Nepal. Still anxious, if possible, to avoid hostilities, Lord Hastings despatched a letter to the Rajah, deprecating the course taken by the Commissioners, and begging that he would no longer delay acceding to our equitable demand. The answer, received on the 4th May 1814, was a direct refusal to resign the lands, which were consequently resumed, the Nepalese troops retiring as ours advanced; police thannas were established, and to prevent exposure to the malaria generated in the Terai during the rainy season, the Military Force was withdrawn, upon which, on the 29th May, the Gorkhas again entered the disputed territories and attacked three of the thannas, killing or wounding most of the Police Officers and murdering in cold blood the thannadar of Chilwah, whom they seized and tied to a tree, when he was deliberately shot with arrows, as an example to deter others from taking service with the British.

This atrocious and unjustifiable act put an end to all further discussion, and could only be construed into an open declaration of war. In order, however, that every avenue to a friendly negotiation might not be finally closed, an opportunity was taken, by the receipt of a letter from the Rajah, to afford him a chance of retracing his steps and averting the consequences of the imprudence and violence of his Councils. A communication, dated 14th June, was therefore addressed to His Highness, pointing out to him the moderation and forbearance which had invariably characterized the proceedings of the British Government, and the prevarication and deceit practised by his own, urging him to exonerate the Durbar from the disgrace of having been accessary to the cowardly murder, which had consummated the attack upon the thannas, by the public and exemplary punishment of the officers concerned in the disgraceful transaction, and, moreover, warning him, that if resolved upon war, he must be prepared to stake the existence of his kingdom on the result. Nothing was gained by this correspondence. After considerable delay, on the 12th August, an evasive and insolent missive was received in reply.

It was now incumbent on the Governor General to make all due preparations for the vigorous prosecution of the war in which we were about to be engaged, and, fortunately, the nobleman at the head of affairs was fully equal to the task which had thus devolved upon him.

It must be remembered, that, at that time, the relative position of the two powers, was vastly different to what it is at present. Whilst we were nearly surrounded by states, if not of known hostility, at all events, of doubtful friendship, and ready to take advantage of any disaster which might happen to our arms; and our territories, stretched for hundreds of miles almost from the Brahmaputra to the Sutledge, exposed to the inroads of the Gorkha troops occupying the lower range of the Himmalayas; not a vulnerable point was apparent throughout their frontier, and we were perfectly ignorant of the enemy we were about to oppose, their natural and artificial means of defence, the Military features of the country, and its political condition and relations.

Valuable information as respects the topography of Nepal, was, however, solicited and obtained from Dr. Hamilton, who had accompanied the Mission in 1803, and other officials who had been employed in the districts bordering the Terai.

Four divisions, as follows, were organized for the invasion of Nepal. The first under the command of General Marley, was directed to assemble on the Sarun frontier, with a view to its moving direct upon the capital by the valley of Mukwanpore, and to the operations of this division, which consisted of 7,989 men, with 26 guns, the Government confidently calculated upon making the most effectual impression upon the enemy.

The second, of 4,698 men, with 12 guns, commanded by General Wood, concentrated at Gorukhpore, and was intended to operate in the direction of Bootwul, and forcing the defile of Nyakot to advance on Tansein, the principal depôt and Military post of the Nepalese in Palpa, thus in a great measure acting as a diversion to the main attack.

The third composed of 10,422 men, with 20 guns, led by General Gillespie, assembled at Saharunpore, for the purpose of penetrating the passes of the Dehrah Dhoon and occupying that valley and other positions in Gurhwal, of seizing the passes of the Jumna and Ganges, so as to prevent the retreat of the enemy's troops stationed to the westward, and of subsequently aiding operations projected against Kemaon, or co-operating with the 4th division.

The fourth, consisted of 7,112 men, with 22 guns, its movements were guided by an officer qualified to meet any emergency, and of whom the Bengal Army may well be proud, General Ochterlony. As a diplomatist, few men could equal him in unravelling the web of chicanery and deception which always envelopes the foreign policy of an oriental court, and, although mild and conciliatory in his manner, he would brook no evasion or prevarication when the interests of his country were concerned, and was prompt to avenge the slightest insult to the British name. As a General, he deemed it a merit to effect more by his own skill as a strategist than by the gallantry of his troops, of which, however, he never failed to avail himself, to the utmost, when necessity demanded. His name is still spoken of with admiration and respect, both by the soldiers he led and the foes he conquered. The force under his guidance was formed of the corps quartered at Kurnaul and Loodianah, in order that it might be launched against the enemy's western army, said to be composed of the flower of their troops.

The defence of the frontier to the eastward of the Kousee river was entrusted to a small force of 2,723 men, under Captain Latter, the Commandant of the Rungpore battalion. General Marley was instructed to move with his Division on Hetoundah *viâ* Bicheeah Khor and the Chiriya Ghati Pass, at the same time, detaching a force to his right to obtain possession of the fort of Hurreehurpore. This having been effected, to mass his troops before the fortress of Mukwanpore, which it was absolutely necessary should fall into our hands before pushing forward to the invasion of the valley of Kathmandhoo; Hetoundah, Mukwanpore and Hurreehurpore were connected by roads easy of access, and would therefore have formed a sound basis for our line of operations, for, with these posts in our hands, little difficulty could have been experienced in acquiring information relative to the practicability of the different paths leading to the capital, and both men and supplies could be readily collected on whatever point might be deemed the most advisable from which to commence the onward march, whilst in the event of a repulse, not only would the line of retreat remain undisturbed, but strong places of arms be afforded to the troops, in which to await the arrival of re-inforcements from the plains. It was left optional with the British commander to select the route by which he might advance after the completion of the operations above detailed, and there can be no doubt that a road could have been discovered, presenting few natural obstacles, which might not have been easily surmounted by British skill and British courage. General Marley arrived on the frontier on the 11th December 1814, in the meantime, the Terai had been cleared of the enemy, by detachments under Colonel Bradshaw and Major Roughsedge, the former attacked and carried the fort of Buhurwa, commanded by Purseram Thapa, who, with 4 other sirdars and 51 sepoys, was killed; many were wounded and taken prisoners, and the fugitives driven across the Bag Mati. The British lost 3 killed and 28 wounded, amongst the latter, Lieutenant Boileau, who received a severe sabre cut in a personal contest with the Subah whom he slew; Chunda Seekha Opadhia, the late wakil of the Rajah, who had taken up his quarters at Buhurwa, surrendered, and the contents of the documents found in his possession, fully revealed the designs of the Durbar, and proved the insincerity of all their protestations as respects their desire that an amicable adjustment should take place of the differences between the States. Had this last success been rapidly followed up, it is not improbable that the valley of Mukwanpore would have been occupied without opposition, unfortunately, the General was ill-qualified for the command of an army destined to act against an active and energetic foe, he delayed advancing until joined by his battering train, the golden opportunity was lost, and the Gorkhas, recovering from the alarm caused by the rapidity of our previous movements, became encouraged to take the initiative, and to project enterprises against our outposts; whilst eventually the successful result of their attacks upon Pursa and Summundpore, which were surprised and almost utterly destroyed on the 1st of January, by overwhelming forces of the enemy,* had so fatal an influence upon the mind of the General, as completely to paralyze the operations of the division under his orders, and occasion—the total failure of every object of its formation.

On the receipt of the intelligence of the defeat of the detachments alluded to in the preceding paragraph, General Marley who was posted at Lowtan, a centrical point about twenty-five miles distant from the scenes of disaster, instead of endeavouring, by some bold and vigorous movement, to restore confidence to his own troops and check the arrogance of the enemy, proceeded towards Bettiah, where he effected his junction with the battering train, and afterwards marched about in different directions, apparently, without any definite purpose. This seeming

* The casualties numbered 381, including 3 officers.

pusillanimity on the part of the British emboldened the enemy; the whole of the Terai again fell into their hands and their incursions even extended into our territories. General Marley, without waiting to be relieved, soon after, relinquished his command, which devolved, in the first instance, upon Colonel Dick, and subsequently upon Major General George Wood, but active operations were suspended and the regiments composing the Division cantoned in position along the line of frontier from the Gunduk to the Kousee, so as to protect the districts of Sarun and Tirhoot, and to present the means of speedily re-uniting at the return of the cold season, subsequent however, to the date, 21st February, of General Wood's assuming charge, a party of Gorkhas were completely discomfited, with the loss of their Chief and a considerable number of men, by a small body of Irregular Cavalry, near Purseram; several stockades were also destroyed.

The destruction of the detachment at Pursa is an instance of the folly of despising an enemy, however contemptible he may appear, a maxim that cannot be too strongly impressed upon the mind of every Military man. The post was situated within the bend of an unfordable nullah, encircling a small fort, and merely required to be isolated by a trench, having a parapet raised above the inner slope, to render it almost impregnable to a foe unaided by skilful artillery. The officer of Pioneers, who accompanied the party to point out the position to be occupied, offered to throw up the necessary works, but the offer was declined. The Gorkhas commenced their attack before day-break, by setting fire to a village at a short distance from the encampment, and which, I believe, contained commissariat supplies. Captain Sibley moved forward with nearly his whole force, consisting of 310 infantry, 50 irregular cavalry and 2 guns, and perhaps anticipated, comparatively speaking, an easy victory; but his troops, from the glare of the burning huts, were fully exposed to the fire of the enemy, who were themselves sheltered by the gloom beyond. Whilst the British were fully engaged to the front, a body of Gorkhas passing round their left flank took possession of their stronghold, the Gurhee; thus completely surrounded, their position became untenable, and although they displayed the greatest gallantry, they were soon overpowered, and obliged to effect a retreat across the nullah, with the loss of their guns and three-fourths of their numbers. The defeat of the troops at Summundpore, which occurred on the same date, was effected almost under identical circumstances. During the campaign a similar attack, but with a different result, was made on a detachment in the Morung; the Officer in command, instead of advancing, took up a position in the rear, firing his tents as he retreated; on the Gorkhas rushing forward into the camp, they suffered from a destructive fire poured in upon them from almost invisible enemies, and ere they could make arrangements for renewing the assault, their casualties were so numerous that they were forced to seek safety in flight; on another occasion also the Nepalese were defeated with great loss in a night attack made upon a picket of 50 men, thrown out from a detachment at Natpur on the Kousee, the Subadar in command had received instructions to retire on the main body (about 2 miles in his rear) in the event of an assault being made on his position, he accordingly retreated in admirable order, finding themselves foiled in their attempt to destroy his party, his opponents taunted him with cowardice, he replied that he merely obeyed orders, almost at that moment the drum of the troops advancing to his support was heard, he immediately halted and called out, My orders are now to fight, come on if ye dare, the Gorkhas not expecting this resistance were defeated and fled, leaving the road strewn with their dead.

The 2nd division assembled at Gorukhpore on the 15th November 1814, but, in consequence of the difficulty and delay experienced in procuring carriage and bearers, was unable to advance until a much later period. Major General J. S. Wood, having occupied the Terai and made suitable arrangements for its defence, proceeded to penetrate the hills in the direction of Bootwul. During his march, however, he received information, which induced him to change the point of attack, and to resolve on forcing a pass to the westward, which, he had reason to believe, would offer a favorable route into Palpa, and enable him to turn the forts by which the Bootwul pass was defended. On the 3rd January 1815, the main body of the force moved to the attack of the redoubt at Jeetgurh; a detachment, under the command of Major Comyn, being directed to turn the left of the enemy's position. Instead of debouching upon a plain in front of the work as the Major General had been led to expect, the troops found themselves exposed to a heavy fire from the stockade, before it was discovered; although the utmost gallantry was displayed, and the Gorkhas to the right of the redoubt driven back, with the loss of their Chief, by the grenadiers, headed by a company of H. M.'s 17th Regiment; perceiving that the work itself was commanded from a hill immediately in its rear, and therefore, if taken, must prove untenable, whilst the fire, in every direction, was extremely galling from parties concealed by the trees, the General was of opinion, that no object would be gained by the further exposure of his men, and a considerable loss having been already sustained, ordered a retreat, which appears to have been conducted with regularity; some ammunition was, however, lost, owing to the majority of the bearers having thrown down their loads. The treacherous guide, by whom the General had been misled, took advantage of the confusion to make his escape through the jungle. After this unsuccessful enterprise, in which our casualties were twenty-four killed and one hundred and ten wounded, General Wood turned his attention to a pass to the eastward of Bootwul, which he did not, however, deem it advisable to attempt in the face of the considerable force with which he conceived the enemy would oppose him; he accordingly moved in a westwardly direction, with the expectation of being able to enter the hills at Toolseepore; but hearing that the Gorkhas, consequent on the absence of his Division, had made inroads into the Company's territories and were plundering the country, and even menacing Gorukhpore, he determined to retrace his steps, and, relinquishing offensive operations, to limit his views to the protection of our own frontier, and the destruction of the crops and villages in the Terai, so as to prevent the enemy deriving any benefit from them during the ensuing campaign. Sickness shortly after broke out amongst his troops, and on the 6th of May, he was under the necessity of breaking up his force, which returned to cantonments.

The conduct of General Wood, in adopting, after his first repulse, a system purely defensive, does not appear to have met with the approbation of the Governor General, who was naturally deeply disappointed at the complete frustration of the design, for the accomplishment of which, this division had been appointed.

The campaign, on the part of the 3rd Division, commenced by the seizure of the Timley Pass, on the 20th October 1814, by Lieutenant Colonel Carpenter, who had been detached for that purpose by Major General Gillespie. On the 24th, the main body entered the Dhoon by the Keree Pass, and marched on Kalunga, while detachments occupied the passes and ferries of the

Jumna, and on the same day the fort of Kalunga was closely reconnoitred by Colonel Mawbey, commanding the advance. Finding it unassailable by the means at his disposal, he relinquished the design of carrying it by a *coup de main*, and awaited the arrival of Head Quarters. On the 30th, under the immediate orders of General Gillespie, the force, formed in four columns, commanded respectively, by Lieutenant Colonel Carpenter, Major Shelly, and Captains Fast and Campbell, with a reserve under Major Ludlow, moved to the attack. The columns were directed to advance from different points, the signal being a gun fired from the batteries, and repeated from the camp below; unfortunately, this signal was not heard either by Major Shelly or Captains Fast and Campbell, and the column under Lieutenant Colonel Carpenter, with the reserve, alone moved forward, and carried in a gallant manner the stockades thrown across the road leading to the fort, pushing on close to the walls; here they were driven back, and forced to take shelter in a village between the first stockade and the fortress, where they were re-enforced by three companies of H. M.'s 53rd Foot, and, led by the General in person, again advanced to the attack, but were again repulsed, after three successive assaults; in the last, General Gillespie, whilst most nobly cheering on his men, when within thirty yards of the gate, received a mortal wound, and fell, sincerely and deeply lamented by the whole army. Our casualties on this occasion were numerous, no less than 225, of whom 20 were officers.

On the failure of this attack, in consequence of the thick jungle in the vicinity of Kalunga rendering it undesirable as a place of encampment, Colonel Mawbey, who succeeded to the command, fell back on Dehrah, about a mile and a half distant, and employed himself in endeavouring to cut off the enemy's supplies of water and provisions, until re-enforced by a battering train from Delhi, on the arrival of which, he resumed his old position, and invested the fort. On the 27th November, a practicable breach having been reported by the officers in charge of the Engineer and Artillery departments, a column, consisting of the Grenadiers of the whole force, with a Battalion Company of H. M.'s 53rd, covered by the Light Company of the same Regiment, and supported by the troops in the trenches, advanced to the assault; most injudiciously, the storming party were directed to proceed with unloaded muskets, and to trust entirely to the bayonet, and their defeat adds one more to the many instances, (in our own army, Whitelock's capitulation at Buenos Ayres,) which have shown the folly of converting the fire arm into a mere lance, and depriving the soldier, not only of its full use, but of the confidence, which the possession of a loaded musket must always inspire. When they reached the head of the breach, they found their further progress barred by a steep descent, further protected by pointed stakes planted along the bottom, whilst they were unable to reply to the showers of stones, spears, arrows and musketry-fire poured in upon them from every direction. With regard to the conduct of a portion of the column, doubts have arisen, but it is certain, that it met with the most strenuous opposition on the part of the Gorkhas; in fact, nothing could exceed the devotion and gallantry they displayed. Every effort made by the British proved of no avail, and after exposure for two hours to a most galling fire, they were obliged to retire, with the heavy loss of 483 men, including 11 officers, killed and wounded.

On the morning of the 30th November, the remnant of the garrison, 70 men, evacuated the fort, and, with their able commander, Bulbuddhur Sing, succeeded in forming a junction with a re-enforcement of about 400 men, and effecting a retreat to the adjacent hills, although closely pursued, and suffering some loss from a detachment commanded by Major Ludlow, who displayed great judgment and gallantry in conducting the pursuit, which was not, however, prosecuted without casualties; three officers, Captain Burke and Ensigns Turner and Richmond, and 16 men being wounded in this affair, in which the sepoys are reported to have behaved with great gallantry. When the British took possession of the fort, the scene of slaughter which everywhere met the eye, fully proved the devoted courage and determined bravery which had been exhibited by the Gorkhas, and established the claim of the defenders of Kalunga to the unqualified esteem and admiration of every true soldier.

The British force pushed on towards Nahun, and, whilst in progress, was joined by Major General Martindell, who assumed the command. Having occupied Nahun, and established magazines and depôts there, the Major General projected a combined movement, with the view of seizing two important positions, situated respectively on the western and eastern sides of the fort of Jyetuk, commanded by Runjore Sing Thapa, by which means he expected to be able to cut off the enemy from their principal watering places, and to intercept their communications with the surrounding country, whence they drew their supplies. Two detachments were accordingly formed, under the command of Majors Ludlow and Richards; the latter, after a fatiguing march, by a circuitous route, reached his destination on the morning of the 27th December, and seized the position he was ordered to occupy. Major Ludlow, with his column, advanced on the same morning to the destined point of attack on the west side of the fort, and, after repulsing the party of Gorkhas opposed to him, and driving them from height to height to a stockaded position in their rear, unfortunately failed in an attempt to carry the stockade, and, the enemy rallying and renewing the contest, our troops were compelled to retire with considerable loss. The miscarriage of the attack conducted by Major Ludlow, induced General Martindell, to send orders to Major Richards to return to camp, vacating the post; in which during the whole day, he had with the utmost resolution, sustained the repeated and vigorous assaults of the enemy, who was enabled, after Major Ludlow's defeat, to turn his whole force against the other detachment. At the close of the day, after the whole of his ammunition was expended, and the troops had been obliged to employ even stones in their defence, Major Richards received the orders to retire, which were executed under cover of a gallant charge made by the Light Company of the first Battalion of the 26th regiment, under Lieutenant Thackeray. A retreat by night through an unknown and difficult country, and in the face of an enemy flushed with success, was necessarily attended with much confusion and heavy loss. Major Ludlow ascribed his failure mainly to the backwardness of a part of his battalion, but with Major Richards' division, the utmost zeal and bravery was evinced by all the troops. Our casualties on this date amounted to 441, including 11 officers.

In consequence of the unsuccessful result of these operations, nothing further was attempted by Major General Martindell until the arrival of re-enforcements early in February; he then took possession of an advanced position in front of Nahun, and opposite to the enemy's principal stockade, which he determined to breach by the fire from a battery, erected on the point thus gained, with the view of subsequently carrying it by assault; however, after it had been levelled to the ground, he conceived that the attack could not be attempted with a prospect of success, and consequently determined to relinquish active operations against the fort, and to effect its reduction by blockade.

In pursuance of this plan General Martindell, after some days, detached a force, under the command of Major Richards, to occupy a position on the eastern side of the fort, near to the post he had seized on the 27th November, in order to intercept the enemy's communications with the country in that direction. Major Richards on his approach to this position encountered a body of the enemy's troops, which had been sent to oppose him, and after a sharp and gallant action, routed the Gorkhas, and pursued them from height to height with considerable loss; the commander of the enemy's party, and several other prisoners, falling into his hands. Major General Martindell successively occupied other positions on different sides of the fort, and gradually effected, in a great degree, the purpose of straitening the enemy, and cutting off his supplies, and there is no reason to doubt, that he would have ultimately compelled him to submit, but in the meantime a negotiation ensued between General Ochterlony and the Nepalese commander, Ummur Sing Thapa, and, under the terms of the capitulation then agreed to, Jyetuk was surrendered to the British force.

The great error committed by General Martindell, and for which his conduct was animadverted on by the Governor General, was, the spirit of vacillation he displayed in carrying out the measures he determined to adopt, and his plans, therefore, although well conceived, in general, owed their ill success solely to the want of determination and energy with which they were put into execution.

The 4th Division, as already mentioned, was formed from the regiments stationed within the Sirhind district, and consisted almost entirely of Native troops. This division penetrated the hills in the direction of Nala Gurh, and on the 4th November opened batteries against that fort, which, with its dependency of Taragurh, surrendered the following day. The casualties in the besieging force only amounted to 7. After establishing depôts at Nala Gurh, General Ochterlony advanced to Ramgurh, and on the 26th November a sharp affair took place, in which a reconnoitring party was driven back by the Gorkhas, with the loss of 1 officer killed and 75 men killed and wounded.

Finding the works occupied by the Gorkhas utterly inaccessible in front, the General moved to their rear, where he took up a secure position, and applied himself to intercepting the enemy's communications with the country and preparing for the attack.

The rugged nature of the country, and the difficulty of making a road passable even for elephants, with the consequent impediments to the transportation of ordnance and stores, rendered this movement, though unopposed, one of uncommon labor. On arriving at the new ground, a spot was selected, from which it was supposed that the guns might be brought to bear upon the enemy's stockades. The battery, however, when erected, proved too distant, and in reconnoitring the ground, in order to choose a more advanced position, the skirmish alluded to in a former paragraph, occurred.

On the 27th December, the Division was re-enforced by the arrival of the second Battalion of the 7th regiment N. I. and the 18-pounders, and, on the same evening, as soon as it was dark, the reserve, under Lieut.-Colonel Thomson, moved to attack a chosen point in the enemy's position, which, after a march of excessive fatigue and difficulty, it reached on the morning of the 28th. Having established himself on the ridge, on which was the work intended to be forced, the Lieut.-Colonel found it necessary to employ Artillery against it, and his field pieces accordingly played upon it, but without much success, during the day. Early next morning he was attacked in his own position by the enemy in considerable force, they were completely repulsed, and immediately afterwards abandoned the stockade, which was taken possession of by our troops. The object of this movement was to effect a lodgment on the ridge between the principal position of the enemy and Belaspore, so as to cut off his communications in that quarter; this, however, was not gained, as the Gorkhas, perceiving the design, frustrated it, by suddenly evacuating all their positions to the left of Ramgurh, and taking up new ground on the opposite side of the fort, which, by a change of front, was still on their right.

Major General Ochterlony continued to keep his attention fixed on the means of intercepting the enemy's supplies, and especially of destroying his direct communications with Belaspore, whence they were chiefly drawn. In accordance with this plan, he marched with the reserve Division, on the 16th of January, across the Gumber river to a point on the road to Irkee and near the southern extremity of the Malown range, having previously detached a strong body of irregulars under Lieutenant Ross, of the 6th regiment, by a circuitous route, with directions to take up a position on the heights above Belaspore, and leaving Lieut.-Colonel Cooper with a battalion and the battering guns strongly stockaded on the old ground at Nher. The result of this manœuvre was, to compel Ummur Sing* to

* This reverse does not appear to have in any way dispirited this able commander, for on the 2nd March he addressed the following remarkable letter to the Rajah of Nepal:—

From Ummer Sing, and his sons Ram Doss and Urjun Thapa, to the Rajah of Nepal, dated Raj Gurh, 2nd March 1815.

A copy of your letter of the 23rd December, addressed to Runjore Sing, under the red seal, was sent by the latter to me, who have received it with every token of respect. It was to the following purport: The capture of Nala Panee by the enemy has been communicated to me from Gurhwal and Kumaon, as also the

quit his position and march to Malown with his whole force, with the exception of

intelligence of his having assembled his force and marched to Nahun. He now occupies the whole country from Barra Pursa to Subtura Muhotree. My army also is secretly posted in various places in the jungles of the mountains. An army under a General has arrived in Goruckpore from Palpa; and another detachment has reached the borders of Beejapore. I have further heard, that a General Officer has set out from Calcutta to create more disturbance. For the sake of a few trifling objects, some intermediate Agents have destroyed the mutual harmony, and war is waging far and wide. All this you knew. You ought to send an Embassy to conciliate the English, otherwise the cause is lost. The enemy, after making immense preparations, have begun the war, and unless great concessions are made, they will not listen to terms. To restore the relations of amity by concession is good and proper. For this purpose, it is fit, in the first place, to cede to the enemy the departments of Bootwul, Palpa, and Sheoraj, already settled by the Commissioners, and the disputed tracts towards Barra. If this be insufficient to re-establish harmony, we ought to abandon the whole of the Terraie, the Dhoon and the Lowlands; and if the English are still dissatisfied, on account of not obtaining possession of a portion of the mountains, you are herewith authorized to give up, along with the Dhoon, the country as far as the Sutleje. Do whatever may be practicable to restore the relations of peace and amity, and be assured of my approbation and assent. If these means be unsuccessful, it will be very difficult to preserve the integrity of my dominions from Khunka Irishta to the Sutleje. If the enemy once obtain a footing in the centre of our territory, both extremities will be thrown into disorder. If you can retire with your army and Military stores, so as to pursue any other plan of operations that may afterwards appear eligible, it will be advisable. On this account, you ought immediately to effect a junction with all the other Officers in the small garrisons left in the forts on the Ramgurh ridge. The stockades thus eva-

western service, and retire to that part of our territory which (including all in your rear as far as Nepal) you may think yourself capable of retaining. These are your orders. In the first place, after the immense preparations of the enemy, he will not be satisfied with these concessions; or if he should accept of our terms, he would serve us as he did Tippoo, from whom he first accepted of an indemnification of six crores of rupees in money and territory, and afterwards wrested from him his whole country. If we were to cede to him so much country he would excite another disturbance at a future opportunity, and seek to wrest from us other provinces. Having lost so much territory, we should be unable to maintain our army on its present footing; and our Military force being once reduced, what means should we have left to defend our eastern possessions? While we retain Boshehur, Gurhwal is secure: if the former be abandoned, the Bhateras of Rewanee will certainly betray us. The English having thus acquired the Dhoon and Rewanee, it will be impossible for us to maintain Gurhwal; and being deprived of the latter, Kamaon and Dootee will also be lost to us. After the seizure of these provinces, Acham, Joomba Dooloo, Duolokh will be wrested from us in succession. You say, that a proclamation has been issued to the inhabitants of the eastern Kurats. If they have joined the enemy, the other Kurats will do so likewise; and then the country, from Dood Koosi on the east, to Bheri on the west, cannot long be retained. Having lost our dominions, what is to *become of our great* Military establishment? When our power is once reduced, we shall have another Knox's Mission, under pretence of concluding a treaty of alliance and friendship, and founding commercial establishments. If we decline receiving their mission, they will insist; and if we are unable to oppose force, and desire them to come unaccompanied with troops, they will not comply. They will begin by introducing a company, a battalion will soon after follow, and at length an army

cuated were seized by a Brigade under Colonel Arnold, who afterwards, in spite

will be assembled for the subjugation of Nepal. Thus you think, that if, for the present, the lowlands, the Dhoon, and the country to the Sutleje were ceded to them, they would cease to entertain designs upon the other Provinces of Nepal. Do not trust them. They who counselled you to receive the mission of Knox, and permit the establishment of a commercial factory, will usurp the Government of Nepal. With regard to the concessions now proposed, if you had, in the first instance, determined upon a pacific line of conduct, and agreed to restore the departments of Bootwul and Sheoraj, as adjusted by the Commissioners, the present contest might have been avoided. But you could not suppress your avarice and desire to retain these places; and having murdered the revenue officer, a commotion arose, and war was waged for trifles. At Jyetuck we have gained a victory over the enemy. If I succeed against Ochterlony, and Runjore Sing with Juspoo Thapa and his Officers prevail at Jyetuck, Runjeet Sing will rise against the enemy, in conjunction with the Seikhs. My army will make a descent into the plains, and our forces, crossing the Jumna from two different quarters, will recover possession of the Dhoon. When we reach Hurdwar, the Nawaub of Lucknow may be expected to take a part in the cause, and on his accession to the general coalition, we may consider ourselves secure as far as Khunka. Relying on your fortune, I trust that Bulbudder Koon and Rowunt Kajee will soon re-enforce the garrison of Jyetuck; and I hope ere long to send Punt Kajee with eight companies, when the forces there will be very strong. The troops sent by you are arriving every day; and when they will come up, I hope we shall succeed both here and at Jyetuck.

Formerly, when the English endeavoured to penetrate to Sindoolee, they continued for two years in possession of Barra Pursa and Mahatree; but when you conquered Nepal, they were either destroyed by your force, or fell victims to the climate, with the

of the inclemency of the weather, which occasioned some delay in the execution of

exception of a few only, who abandoned the place. Orders should now be given to all your officers to defend Choundinde and Choundund in Beejapore, the two Kurats, and the ridge of Mahabharut. Suffer the enemy to retain the lowlands for a couple of years; measures can afterwards be taken to expel them. Lands transferred under a written agreement cannot again be resumed; but if they have been taken by force, force may be employed to recover them. Fear nothing, even though the Seikhs should not join us. Should you succeed now in bringing our differences to an amicable termination, by the cession of territory, the enemy in the course of a few years would take possession of Nepal, as he did the country of Tippoo. The present is, therefore, not the time for treaty and conciliation. These expedients should have been adopted before the murder of the revenue officer, or must be postponed till victory shall crown our efforts.' If they will then accede to the terms which I shall propose, it is well: if not, it will be my business, with the favor of God, and your fortune and country, to preserve the integrity of my country from Khunka to the Sutleje. Let me entreat you, therefore, never to make peace. Formerly, when some individuals urged the adoption of a treaty of peace and commerce, I refused my assent to that measure; and I will not now suffer the honour of my Prince to be sullied by concession and submission. If you are determined on this step, bestow the humiliating office on him who first advised it: but for me, call me to your presence. I am old, and only desire once more to kiss your feet. I can recollect the time when the Gorkha army did not exceed twelve thousand men. Through the favor of heaven, and the renown of your forefathers, your territory was extended to the confines of Khunka on the east. Under the auspices of your father we subjugated Kamaon, and through your fortune we have pushed our conquests to the Sutleje. Four generations have been employed in the acquisition of all this dignity and dominion.

the movement, marched to Ruttungurh, thus commanding the principal line of com-

At Nala Paneo, Bulbuddor cut up three or four thousand of the enemy: at Jyetuck, Runjore Sing with his officers overthrew three battalions. In this place I am surrounded and daily fighting with the enemy and look forward with confidence to victory. All the inhabitants and Chiefs of the country have joined the enemy. I must gain two or three victories before I can accomplish the object I have in view of attaching Runjeet Sing to our cause. On his accession and after the advance of the Seikhs and Gorkhas towards the Jumna, the Chiefs of the Deccan may be expected to join the coalition, as also the Nowaub of Lucknow and the Salih Ramoe Saudh. Then will be the time for us to drive out the enemy, and recover possession of the low countries of Palpa as far as Beejapore. If we succeed in regaining these, we can attempt further conquests in the plains. There has been no fighting in your quarter yet. The Cheundinde and Choundund of Beejapore, as far as the ridge of Mahabharut and Selleanah, should be well defended. Countries acquired in four generations under the administration of the Thapas, should not be abandoned, for the purpose of bringing matters to an amicable adjustment, without deep and serious reflection. If we are victorious in the war we can easily adjust our differences; and if we are defeated, death is preferable to reconciliation on humiliating terms. When the Chinese army invaded Nepal, we implored the mercy of Heaven, by offerings to the Brahmins, and the performance of religious ceremonies; and through the favor of one, and the intercession of the other, we succeeded in repulsing the enemy. Ever since you confiscated the Jagirs of the Brahmins, thousands have been in distress and poverty. Promises were given, that they should be restored on the capture of Kangra, and orders to this effect under the red seal, were addressed to me and Nya Sing Thapa. We failed, however, in that object, and now there is an universal commotion; you ought, therefore, to assemble the Brahmins, and promise to restore

munication between Malown and Belaspore. Lieutenant Ross also took up the

to them their lands and property, in the event of your conquering and expelling the English. By those means, many thousand respectable Brahmins will put up their prayers for our protection, and the enemy will be driven forth. By the practice of charity the territory acquired in four generations may be preserved, and through the favor of God, our power and dominion may be still further extended. By the extension of territory, our Military establishment may be maintained on its present footing, and even increased. The numerous countries which you propose to cede to the enemy yielded a revenue equal to the maintenance of an army of four thousand men, and Kangra might have been captured. By the cession of these provinces, the fear of your name and the splendour of your Court will no longer remain. By the capture of Kangra your name would have been rendered formidable; but though that has not happened, a powerful impression has nevertheless been made on the people of the plains, by the extension of our conquest to the Sutleje. To effect a reconciliation by the cession of the country to the west of the Jumna, would give rise to the idea that the Gorkhas were unable to oppose the English, would lower the dignity of your name in the plains, and cause a reduction in your army to the extent of four thousand men. The enemy will, therefore, acquire possession of Beshehur, and after that the conquest of Gurhwal will be easy: nor will it be possible, in that case, for us to retain Kamaon; and with it we must lose Dootee, Acham, and Joomba. He may be expected to penetrate even to Bhoree. If the English once establish themselves firmly in possession of a part of the hills, we should be unable to drive them out. The countries towards the Sutlejo should be obstinately defended: the abandonment of the disputed tracts in the plains is a lesser evil. The possession of the former preserves to us a road to further conquests. You ought, therefore, to direct Gooroo Runguath Pundit and Dulbhunjur Pandre to give up the disputed lands of

position assigned him, after defeating a body of the Belaspore troops. The suc-

Bootwul, Sheeraj, and the twenty-two villages in the vicinity of Barra, and, if possible, bring our differences to a termination. To this step I have no objections, and shall feel no animosity to those who may perform the service. I must, however, declare a decided enmity to such as, in bringing about a reconciliation with the English, consult only their own interests, and forget their duty to you.

If they will not accept the terms, what have we to fear? The English attempted to take Bhurtpore by storm: but the Rajah Runjeet Sing destroyed a European regiment and a battalion of sepoys. To the present day they have not ventured to meddle with Bhurtpore, and one fort has sufficed to check their progress. In the low country of Dharma (perhaps Bhurma) they established their authority; but the Rajah overthrew their army, and captured all their artillery and stores, and now continues in the quiet possession of his dominions. Our proffers of peace and reconciliation will be interpreted as the result of fear, and it would be absurd to expect that the enemy will respect a treaty concluded under such circumstances. Therefore, let us confide our fortunes to our swords, and by boldly opposing the enemy, compel him to remain within his own territory; or if he should continue to advance, stung with shame at the idea of retreating after his immense preparations, we can then give up the lands in dispute and adjust our differences. Such, however, is the fame and terror of our swords, that Bulbudder, with a nominal force of six hundred men, but scarcely amounting to five hundred, destroyed an army of three or four thousand English. His force consisted of the old Gorkha and Burukh companies (which were only partly composed of the inhabitants of our ancient kingdom), and of the people of the countries from Bheri to Gurhwal, and with these he destroyed one battalion and crippled and repulsed another. My army is similarly composed; nevertheless, all descriptions

cessive reduction of the forts on the Ramgurh range was yet to be accomplished; this

are eager to meet the enemy. In your quarter you are surrounded by the veterans of our army, and therefore cannot apprehend desertions among them: you have also an immense militia and many Jagirdars, who will fight for their own honor and interests. Assembling the militia of the low lands and fighting in the plains is impolitic: call them into the hills and cut them up by detail. (A passage here, the sense of which cannot be discovered.) The enemy is proud and flushed with success, and has reduced under his subjection all the western zemindars, the Ranahs and Rajahs of Kurnaul and the Takhoorae, and will keep peace with no one. However my advice is nothing. I will direct Ram Doss to propose to General Ochterlony the abandonment on our part of the disputed lands, and will forward to you the answer which he may receive. All the Rajahs, Ranahs *and* Takhoorae have joined the enemy, and I am surrounded. Nevertheless we shall fight and conquer; and all my officers have taken the same resolution. The Pundits have pronounced the month of Bysack as particularly auspicious for the Gorkhas, and by selecting a fortunate day we shall surely conquer. I am desirous of engaging the enemy slowly and with caution, but cannot manage it, the English being always in a desperate hurry to fight. I hope, however, to be able to delay the battle till Bysack, when I will choose a favorable opportunity to fight them. When we shall have driven the enemy from hence, either Runjore Sing or myself, according to your wishes, will repair to your presence. In the present crisis it is very advisable to write to the Emperor of China, to the Lama of Lassa, and to the other Lamas; and for this purpose I beg to submit the enclosed draft of a letter* to their address; any errors in it will, I trust, be forgiven by you, and I earnestly recommend that you lose no time in sending a petition to the Emperor of China and a letter to the Lama.

* In this letter the Gorkhas are styled tributaries and dependants of the Emperor of China.

operation, which was one of considerable difficulty, owing to the nature of the country, occupied a period of about six weeks of incessant exertion, and it was not until the 1st of April that Lieut.-Col. Cooper's detachment, to whom the duty had been allotted, was placed in its appointed position before Malown. Posts were now established commanding all the avenues leading to Ummur Sing's line of works, by which he was much straitened. In conducting these operations, a check was experienced by a body of irregulars occupying a strongly stockaded post, a sally was made by the Gorkhas, and this party being found off its guard, suffered severely, and the stockades were destroyed; the disaster was, however, soon repaired. On the 14th and 15th of April, a combined attack was concerted on the enemy's chain of positions, which was carried into effect with the most complete success, the line being penetrated in several points. On the morning of the 16th, a desperate assault was made by the whole of the Gorkha force, headed by their principal Commanders, Ummur Sing and Bhugtie Thapa, on the post occupied by the reserve, in which they were repulsed with considerable loss; the latter Sirdar being amongst the slain. After this defeat they concentrated their troops in Malown, and the detached works forming a part of its defences. The fighting during the 15th and 16th was most severe and the British casualties were numerous, 64 killed and 292 wounded, including amongst the former, 2, and the latter, 4 officers. It was on this occasion that an instance of intrepid gallantry was displayed by Lieutenant Cartwright, of the artillery, who, when the desperate perseverance of the enemy had left him with only one man unwounded, with that one man continued to serve his gun.

The effects of this success were soon observed in the increasing distress of the enemy, and in numerous desertions which evinced the depression of spirits suffered by the garrison, approaches were now pushed forward against the fort, and possession having been obtained of one of the outworks, the whole of the remainder were abandoned by their defenders, who came over in a body to the British camp, leaving Ummur Sing confined to his stronghold, with a garrison reduced to about two hundred men, but all the outworks, stockades and redoubts having been occupied by our troops, his surrender became inevitable, negotiations ensued, in the course of which, however, no relaxation occurred in the preparations for battering the fortress, and on the 15th of May, the Gorkha commander, after having, throughout the campaign, shewn the utmost gallantry and skill, capitulated, on the following terms.

1st. That all the forts and possessions of the Gorkhas, west of the Jumna, should be immediately surrendered to the British troops.

2nd. That orders for the evacuation of all the forts and possessions of the Gorkhas in Gurhwal should be immediately despatched to the commanders in that quarter, and that the troops should be permitted to retire by the Kemaon route across the Kali.

3rd. That Ummur Sing with the remaining garrison of Malown should be permitted to retire across the Kali, with their arms, private baggage and families, and with two guns.

4th. That Runjore Sing should be permitted in like manner, with two hundred men of the garrison of Jyetuk and with one gun, and three hundred unarmed followers, to retire across the Kali.

These arrangements having been concluded and the forts surrendered, the necessary measures were adopted for breaking up the divisions employed before Malown and Jyetuk, and remanding the corps to their respective stations. Throughout the arduous war in which he had been engaged, the proceedings of General Ochterlony had been marked by a combination of foresight, prudence, sagacity, perseverance and professional ability, with energetic promptness in action, which earned for him the unqualified thanks of the Government; every praise is also due to the gallant troops who so successfully carried out the able designs of their commander, at an altitude of about 8,000 feet, unprovided with suitable camp equipage, sutringees flung across bambus officiating for tents, and as respects the sepoys, even deficient in clothing, for they were without pantaloons or great coats, cheerfully enduring the hardships of an Alpine winter, and, notwithstanding the opposition of the elements, wresting from the hardy and resolute mountaineers, the whole of their formidable positions in that quarter of the Himmalayas.

Whilst the operations above described were being carried on, the enemy's territories in Kemaon had not been allowed to remain undisturbed, in the first instance, owing to the paucity of troops of the line, an irregular force of about 4,000 men, with 4 guns, was appointed for this service, and the command given to Lieutenant-Colonel Gardner, an officer of known ability, having under his orders, Captain Hearsey, another local officer of talents and experience. In consequence of bad weather, this force did not enter the hills before the 15th of February; having seized the Chilkeeah pass, it advanced by a route lying chiefly along the line of the Kousillah river. The enemy retired towards Almorah, closely pursued by Colonel Gardner, who ultimately took up a position at Katar Mul. In the advance, several skirmishes took place, in which the irregulars behaved well and always gained the advantage; but a detachment employed in the siege of Kuttoolgurh, under Captain Hearsey, was defeated, and its leader taken prisoner.

It was now determined to collect a regular force, for the purpose of supporting and completing the operations so happily commenced by Lieut.-Colonel Gardner. A Brigade of 2,025 Native Infantry, with 10 guns, was accordingly formed, and Colonel Nicolls, Quarter Master General, King's troops, entrusted with the command.

Colonel Nicolls arrived at Katar Mul on the 8th of April, and as soon as the troops were assembled, a detachment under the command of Major Patton, 5th regiment N. I., was ordered to seize a post situated to the north-west of Almorah. Major Patton having come up with the enemy, instantly attacked him in his position, and after a conflict, in which the sepoys behaved with much gallantry, completely routed and dispersed his opponents with considerable loss, their commander, Husteh Dul, being killed, whilst the casualties on the side of the British were only 28, including 1 officer.

This defeat and the death of their principal Sirdar, produced an impression on the minds of the enemy's troops of which Colonel Nicolls took advantage, and on the 25th of April, he attacked and carried by assault the fortified heights and town of Almorah; during the night an attempt was made by the Gorkhas to recover the position from which they had been driven; but although the attack was conducted with extraordinary resolution, they were effectually beaten back; the loss experienced during these operations was 211, including 3 officers, killed and wounded. The enemy being now convinced of the futility of offering further resistance to the British troops, proposed terms of surrender, and a convention was accordingly soon after concluded, under the provisions of which, they evacuated the province and retired across the Kali; the highest commendation being awarded to Colonel Nicolls, for the distinguished skill and gallantry with which the movements of his force had been directed.

I have already stated that the defence of the northern frontier, east of the Kousee, had been assigned to a detachment under Captain Latter, this officer displayed much judgment and energy in carrying out the purpose with which he had been entrusted, and not only thoroughly secured the safety of our own possessions, but deprived the enemy of a considerable portion of the Morung district.

Thus, notwithstanding the disasters which clouded the commencement of hostilities, and the failure of some of the principal divisions to accomplish the objects for which they were designed, the progress and result of the campaign was highly honorable to our arms, terminating in the expulsion of the Gorkhas from the whole country to the west of the Kali, and the annexation to the British dominions of the important province of Kemaon, with an extensive, fertile and valuable tract in the Terai.

Negotiations were now opened with the Durbar; the loss of so large a portion of their hill territory, having, at last, convinced the Chiefs of the danger to be incurred by continued resistance to the British Power, and naturally weakened their confidence of security behind their mountain barriers, which they had hitherto deemed impregnable. In suing for peace, no stigma could attach to the Sirdars; throughout the arduous struggle in which they had been engaged, they had invariably displayed the utmost gallantry and devotion, and fully maintained the national reputation for undaunted bravery;* somewhat, however, tarnished in the early part of the war, by a dastardly attempt to

* The Gorkhas on several occasions charged up to the Bayonets even of our European Troops, and in the personal contests which took place between the Sirdars and our Officers, instances I believe have been known, of their deliberately sacrificing their lives in order to cut down their opponents, on finding their knives an unequal match against our swords.

destroy the British troops, by poisoning the water of the wells and tanks, by a vegetable poison known under the names of mitha, mohoor, umrit or khet bish, several bags and wicker baskets containing this deleterious substance having been discovered and produced to our officers.

With a force (exclusive of a rude and hastily collected militia, courageous indeed and hardy, but ill-trained, and without discipline) never exceeding 16,000 men,* they had opposed and in many points successfully resisted, an invasion undertaken by a British army, numbering at one period 49,077, of whom no less than 4,557 were European troops.

On the 28th May 1815 Guru Gugraj Mishar, a person known to be decidedly friendly to the maintenance of amicable relations between the two States, and who,

* Their regular Force was estimated as follows:—West of the Jumna 4,000, between the Jumna and Kali 2,000, east of the Kali 6,000=12,000.

subsequent to the demise of Rajah Rana Bahadur, to whom he had officiated as family priest, had resided at Benares, and only recently returned to Kathmandhoo, arrived in Lieutenant-Colonel Bradshaw's camp, accompanied by Chunda Seekha Opadhia, and produced a paper under the Rajah's red seal, empowering him to bring to an adjustment all depending matters between the two Governments, and declaring whatever he engaged for, should be confirmed. The terms proposed by the Governor General were sufficiently stringent, comprehending the perpetual cession of all the hill country taken in the campaign, and, as well as such parts of the low land as were in dispute before the war, of the whole line of Terai to the very foot of the hills, and a fort and territory which had been seized from the Sikhim Rajah previous to the breaking out of hostilities with the British, but which we deemed ourselves pledged to restore, having formed an alliance with that

Chief and taken him under our protection; it was also stipulated that a Resident should be received at Kathmandhoo. These conditions having been communicated to the Guru, he at once declared his inability to treat on this basis, and broke off negotiations, stating that he did not possess authority to comply with such extensive demands, and that sacrifices of such magnitude were not contemplated by the Durbar, as justly arising from the events or actual state of the war. Anxious for an accommodation of affairs and with the hope of obtaining more favorable conditions from other negotiators, a second overture was made by the Gorkha Government through the late Chief of Almorah, the Chountra Bum Sah, who was in communication with the Honourable Edward Gardner, the British commissioner for the management of the conquered province; several conferences took place, but although the discussion was conducted by Mr. Gardner with much judgment and ability, the negotiations in this quarter also terminated unsatisfactorily.

In August, the Guru, who had remained in Lieut.-Col. Bradshaw's camp, received further instructions from his court, and, as the general tenor of the language and proceedings of the Nepal Government appeared to indicate a more favorable disposition than had been previously evinced, negotiations were renewed. Apparently the main objection to the cession of the Terai was, that most of the principal Sirdars enjoyed considerable jagirs in that territory, the Marquis of Hastings was therefore so far induced to modify the terms of the treaty, as to offer the grant of similar possessions or of an equivalent in money pensions, to the amount of two or three lacs of rupees, the distribution to be left at the uncontrolled pleasure of the Durbar; he even determined, though not without reluctance, to waive the stipulation for the mutual reception of accredited agents, if it should appear that the

Gorkha Government was very adverse to that provision. The conduct of the Nepal negotiators was again marked by an extraordinary degree of vacillation, indicative either of fear, or inability to confirm the basis conceded by the Rajah's letters, and in September, negotiations were again brought to a close, the Guru declaring that the Chiefs would never accede to the surrender of the Terai, which was alleged to be the main source of their subsistence, the hills themselves being comparatively unproductive. From this it was evident that the demand for the Terai was a bar to the re-establishment of peace, which no advantage that we might propose could compensate to the Nepal Government, whilst it was insisted upon by the British, rather from a sense of honor and a desire to visit with marked severity the act of gross violence and insult, which had arisen out of former disputes about the low lands, than from any expectation of deriving from them an increase of revenue, the Supreme Government therefore, balancing the advantage of a restoration of peace against the gratification of forcing on the Gorkhas the sacrifice of an object extremely valuable to them, resolved upon relaxing the vigour of the original demand.

A draft of a revised treaty was accordingly transmitted to Lieut.-Col. Bradshaw, to be delivered openly to the Guru, in case of his expected re-appearance with a fresh overture, accompanied by a declaration, that it contained the only conditions on which the Governor General was willing to make peace. In this draft, the Terai from the Kali to the Gunduk, and of the rest, only that portion which was in our actual possession, was insisted on. On the 10th of October, this document was submitted to the Guru and Chunda Seekha Opadhia, but on becoming acquainted with its purport, they at once asserted, that they could not conclude a treaty on the terms proposed, and requested that a delay of fifteen days might be allowed, to admit of a reference on the subject being made to the Rajah, promising that a definitive answer should be given within that period. This request was of course acceded to, but, at the expiration of the prescribed time no instructions had been received, and it was also ascertained that the offer to assign pensions to the Chiefs deprived of their jagirs in the territory proposed to be surrendered, had caused great dissatisfaction, it being represented, which was truly the case, that it would be extremely impolitic to sanction an arrangement, by which many of the principal Sirdars would have become stipendiaries of a Foreign Power, and consequently to a great extent its dependants. At the head of the dissenting party stood Ummur Sing and his sons, who had opposed the commencement of the war as promising little success, but now that it had been begun, were of opinion, that it should be carried on to the last extremity. Many apologies were made by the Guru and his colleague for their failure to redeem their pledge; they even offered to sign the treaty provisionally, if a portion of the Terai were substituted for the money payment, and urged Lieut.-Col. Bradshaw to consent to a further delay. This was, however, declined, and negotiations ceased, but on the 29th October the Nepalese negotiators left for Kathmandhoo, declaring that they would return within 12 days with the treaty duly signed. On the 28th November the Guru arrived at Segowlee and signed the treaty according to the draft submitted to his Court, by the terms of which, the ratification of the Rajah was to be delivered within 15 days. On being apprised of this event, the Supreme Government, with a view to conciliate the Chiefs, and shew generosity towards a fallen and suppliant foe, determined to make further concessions, but, at the expiration of the appointed period the ratified treaty had not been delivered, and it was discovered, not only that it would not be produced, but that active preparations were in progress for renewed hostility, and positions already taken up in the Terai by the Gorkha troops, who, presuming upon their former success over the divisions employed upon the Gorukhpore and Sarun frontier during the previous campaign, trusted, owing to the delay which they expected would occur ere negotiations were finally terminated, to be enabled to baffle the attack of the British troops, until the setting in of the rainy season might compel the latter to return to their cantonments, and thus to protract the contest for another year, during which period they hoped to succeed in gaining more favorable terms than those now granted. Throughout the rains, a large body of troops had been held in readiness in Bahar, and at the close of them, General Ochterlony had been summoned from the north-west to assume the command, preparatory to an advance upon Kathmandhoo as soon as the passage of the forest might be practicable. Unfortunately, upon the signature of the treaty, the activity of preparation had been a little relaxed; more especially in the commissariat department, and consequently, when war became inevitable, it was feared that some delay must occur ere the troops would be prepared to take the field. On the 5th January 1816, Major General Ochterlony was made acquainted with the unexpected result of the negotiations conducted by Lieut.-Colonel Bradshaw, and directed to join the force on the frontier, for the purpose of prosecuting active operations against the Gorkhas; he was at the same time invested with exclusive powers to direct all political negotiations and arrangements with relation to the Government of Nepal. Owing to extraordinary exertion in every department, Civil and Military, before the end of the month, the army was in readiness for a forward movement, and on the 25th, the General arrived in camp at Bhulloa and assumed the command. On the 9th of February, after throwing up a stockaded work at Simra Basa, he advanced, with an Infantry Brigade and 8 guns, to Bichceah Khor, passing the forest without opposition. On the 14th, the Guru and Chunda Seekha were admitted to a final interview; but, not being possessed of the ratified treaty, the propositions they submitted were declared inadmissible. All further discussion was at once suspended, the negotiators dismissed, and the war recommenced with the utmost vigor and activity.

The army now employed by the British Government to enforce their demands against the Nepal Durbar, and cause in future on the part of that crafty Court, a proper observance of the respect due to our power in India, numbered 33,446 men, with a large force of Artillery. It was divided into four divisions as follows:—The first, under General Ochterlony, assembled near Segowlee, and consisted of 19,394 of all ranks. The second, commanded by Colonel J. Nicolls, was collected at Seetapore in Oude, with a view to the invasion of the provinces of Dootee, Acham and Saliana, and mustered 6,617. The third of 4,946, was merely intended as a corps of observation, to be employed under Major General J. S. Wood, on the Gorukhpore frontier; and the fourth, which ought rather to be styled a detachment, its strength being only 2,489, was placed under the orders of Captain Latter, for the purpose of invading the Morung province. The principal division advanced in three columns; the right, under Colonel Kelly, H. M.'s 24th, moving, by the Bag Mati route, on Hurreehurpore, and the left, under Colonel Nicolls, H. M.'s 66th, to the westward of the main body, by the valley of the Raptee, the former, being concentrated at Bhugwanpore, and the latter, at Ramnuggur.

Due precautions having been taken for the safety of the different posts in the rear and protecting the line of communication, on the 14th February, Colonel Miller's Brigade, (attached to the main column,) led by the General in person, moved forward at 9 P. M. by a route discovered by Captain Pickersgill, of the Quarter Master General's department, and which was still unknown to the enemy; the path ran through a precipitous and narrow ravine, called Balee Kolee, and thence by a watercourse leading to a steep acclivity by which the first formidable barrier of hills was to be carried; the march was continued the whole night, and by 8 in the morning, the Chiriya range of hills, to the west of the Gorkha position, was occupied, without resistance, by the light company of the advance, yet so difficult was the ascent, that it was not accomplished by the whole of the troops before sunset. In the course of the 15th, the Brigade advanced about 5 miles to the Chukka Mukka nullah, situated to the north of the range, and within 1 coss of the Raptee, where it bivouacked for 4 days, waiting the arrival of provisions and tents. Nothing could exceed the patience with which the toil and privations of this march were endured by the troops, many of whom were for 2 days wholly without food; the rapidity of the movement, added to the ruggedness of the ground, rendering it impossible to bring up supplies.

Whilst these operations were in progress, Colonel Burnett, with the 4th Brigade, pushed on to the entrance of the Chiriya Ghati pass; on a reconnoisance having been made, it was discovered that the first stockade had been deserted by the enemy, who also evacuated the second, on the approach of our reconnoitring party, which was thus enabled to proceed almost to the summit of the pass, where, however, it was received by a heavy, though ill-directed fire from the heights, and obliged to fall back, with the loss of 1 man killed and 8 wounded, amongst the latter, Lieut. Walcott, of the artillery.

On the morning of the 17th, it was ascertained that the enemy had retired, owing to the successful movement on their flank, and the pass was therefore occupied without opposition. On the 19th, General Ochterlony marched to Hetoundah, where works were thrown up for the protection of the depôt, which it was intended should be established at that post.

Having provided for the defence of Hetoundah, the force moved on the 27th towards Mukwanpore, taking up a position on an open level ground in a southwardly direction, and about two miles distant from the hills covering the fortified heights and detached defences of that Fortress: the following morning it was joined by the battering train and Lieutenant-Colonel Burnett's brigade, and on the afternoon of the same date, an attack was made by the Gorkhas on a detached post, called Sekha Khutree, situated on a hill to the left of the camp. The approach of large bodies of the enemy having been observed by General Ochterlony, about 1 P. M., he successively detached to the aid of the party on the hills, 3 companies H. M.'s 87th regiment, the 2d battalion 25th regiment N. I., 2d battalion 12th N. I., with 2 guns, and the 2d battalion 8th N. I.

The number of the enemy was estimated at not less than 2,000 men, with several guns, and during the conflict they repeatedly re-ceived re-enforcements. During a momentary superiority, they approached close to the village, which was obstinately and gallantly disputed by our small detachment, until the arrival of more troops changed the fortune of the day; and from this time until half-past 5, their repeated assaults on our position were invariably repulsed, and they were at length driven off in confusion, chiefly by a charge of the 2d battalion of the 8th regiment N. I. in the direction of the enemy's guns, one of which, a 4-pounder, on a mountain train carriage, was abandoned. The British casualties on this occasion were numerous, 222, including 2 officers. The loss of the enemy, by their own subsequent acknowledgment, exceeded 800. In the mean time the left column had crossed the ridge by the Bheekunnee pass, and moved forward, without experiencing any opposition, by the valley of the Raptee to Hetoundah, leaving 2 native battalions, with their proportion of field guns, at Ekore, under Major Lumley, with the view of checking any attempt on the part of the enemy from their posts at Kadrung and Oopudurung, to which they had retired on its advance. Colonel Kelly, with the light column, marching by the course of the Bag Mati, arrived before Hurreehurpore, on the 29th February; it appearing that a strong point within about 800 yards of one of the Gorkha stockades had been unoccupied, it was determined to seize it, and a detachment, under Lieutenant-Colonel O'Halloran, was ordered to advance for this purpose the next morning, at 3 o'clock; it consisted of 2 companies of each of the following regiments: H. M.'s 24th, 18th N. I., Chumparun Light Infantry, and 1 company 2d battalion 21st regiment N. I., with two 3-pounders, conveyed by bearers; and carried the position a little before 6 A. M., dislodging a picquet, left for its protection. The enemy, in very considerable force, made a most desperate and obstinate attempt to recover this point, and a re-enforcement was despatched by Colonel Kelly to cover the rear of the post, which was threatened. It was impossible, from the nature of the ground, to close, or use the bayonet, and the musketry continued without intermission until half-past 11 o'clock, when the arrival of two 6-pounders and two $5\frac{1}{2}$-inch howitzers, on elephants, in a few minutes decided the affair, and left the British in possession of an almost natural redoubt, very advantageously situated for further operations. This success was not, however, gained without some loss, 59, including 5 officers, being killed and wounded. After this repulse, the Gorkhas became apparently disheartened, and on the morning of the 4th March, during a storm of rain, evacuated the fort and hill.

From the date of the arrival of General Ochterlony at Hetoundah, although he had received no direct overtures on the part of the Nepalese authorities, yet it was evident that a desire for peace pervaded the minds of many of the Sirdars, at the same time, they still clung to the hope that fortune might so far favor them as to enable the campaign to be protracted until the setting in of the rainy season, when they might reasonably presume that the British Government would feel disposed to offer terms somewhat less stringent than those now submitted for their acceptance. On the 25th February, Chunda Seekha had an interview with the General, when, as an inducement to delay the advance of the force, he alluded to the expected arrival of the Guru, for the purpose of concluding the war by an amicable settlement of affairs; he was, however, distinctly informed, that the onward movement of the British would not be for a moment deferred owing to the re-opening of negotiations; thus, all their endeavours to obtain a suspension of hostilities having been frustrated, and the intelligence of their reverses at Sekha Khutree and Hurreehurpore having spread consternation at Kathmandhoo, the Durbar immediately resolved, to make a tender of unqualified submission, as the only means of averting the most disastrous consequences.

The Red Seal having been hurriedly affixed to the treaty of Segowlee it was dispatched to the Gorkha Commander, Kazi Bactour Sing, one of their principal Sirdars, who, on the 3rd March, wrote to the General, to mention that he had the instrument in his possession and would forward it by Chunda Seekha. In reply, he was informed, that the Gorkha Government must not now expect the same terms as before the re-commencement of the war; but, in the event of the Brahman's being furnished with full powers, he would be received. In the interim, approaches were pushed to within 500 yards of the defences of Mukwanpore, and a battery thrown up in readiness to open upon the fort, Chunda Seekha soon made his appearance with the ratified treaty, which, in the most submissive, and even abject manner, he earnestly pressed upon the General's acceptance. After a discussion of some length, in which he dwelt upon the dissimulation, evasion and bad faith, which had marked the conduct of the Nepalese Government; having ascertained that the spirit of hostility was completely annihilated, and deeming the foe sufficiently humbled, Sir David Oehterlony, after keeping the envoy in eonsiderable suspense, at last listened to his entreaties, and agreed to accept the treaty, explaining to Chunda Seekha, that whatever disposition the Supreme Government might have had, before the late operations, to extend its bounty to the Nepalese beyond the letter of the engagement, no favor could be now expeeted, and the negotiator was, aecordingly, called upon, to give a speeific note in writing, declaratory of his having no such hopes; together with an assuranee that a similar deelaration should be made in a letter from the Rajah to the Governor General. This was readily agreed to, and the contest with the Nepalese was thus finally terminated in the beginning of March, and the requisite orders for a retrograde movement at onee issued to the leaders of the different columns engaged in the campaign.

The provisions of the treaty differed little from the terms already stated in a previous paragraph; one of the conditions, however, not hitherto mentioned, was the agreement, that no British subject, nor the subject of any European or American State, should be permitted to enter the Gorkha service, without the sanction of the British Government having been previously obtained. The articles were punctually executed by the Gorkhas; but the Governor General, notwithstanding what had passed, deeming that it would be a politic act of conciliation, to cede, in lieu of pensions now stipulated, such of the Terai, as had been before contemplated, gave notice to the Durbar of his intention to send the Hon'ble E. Gardner as Resident, and to empower him to conclude an arrangement on such a basis, and this settlement was subsequently carried into effect.

A treaty was, at the same time, concluded with the Rajah of Sikhim, of somewhat similar a nature; it, however, embraces a stipulation for the surrender of dacoits, revenue defaulters and other delinquents who may seek refuge within his territories.

The Gorkhas had shown themselves in the course of the campaign a most gallant foe and as formidable an enemy as any then existing in India; the conditions of the peace now concluded, were, however, well calculated to undermine their power; as not only were their resources weakened and their dominions curtailed, but by our possession of the mountains to the west of the Gogra, and the position obtained to the east, by the protection afforded to the Sikhim Rajah, in the event of a future war, both their flanks would be fully exposed to our attacks, whilst, almost the whole of their regular force would be required to oppose the powerful army, which would doubtless be concentrated on the Gorukhpore and Sarun frontier, in order to force a passage to the valley of Kathmandhoo, by some of the numerous passes in that direction.

CHAPTER VI.

Origin of the Feuds between the Pundees and Thapas—Succession of Maha Rajah Rajindra Bikram Sah—Deposition from office and suicide of Bheem Sing Thapa—Nomination of a Member of the Pundee Family as Minister—Return to power of the Thapa Faction—Murder of Mahtabar Sing—Coalition of the adverse parties—Assassination of Guggun Sing—Massacre of the Kot—Appointment to the Wizarat of Jung Bahadur—Flight of the King to Benares—Installation of his successor—Defeat and captivity of the Ex-Monarch—Object of the Mission to England—Life of Jung Bahadur—His Character.

THE unsuccessful result of their presumption in measuring arms with the British, effectually curbed the ambition of the Nepalese, and with the exception of occasional endeavours to subjugate some of the tribes to the north-east, in which they have but partially succeeded, they have since refrained from any attempt to increase their territory, in fact, the Chiefs seem to have been fully occupied in carrying on the internal feuds, which appear to have had their origin from the date of the return, from Benares, of Rajah, Rana Bahadur. Previous to that event, a large portion of the authority of the Government was vested in the hands of the Pandee Family, the head of whom, Damodar Pandee, who had been mainly instrumental in securing the Monarch's abdication, and subsequently, during the Regency of the Rani, had exercised considerable influence over her councils, was with his son condemned to death, on the re-assumption of sovereignty by the Rajah; and, as their execution was generally ascribed to the instigation of the young favorite, Bheem Sing Thapa, from that time, the Pandees and Thapas have been antagonistic factions. There is another party, the Chountras, offshoots from Royalty, who have also long enjoyed great power, and sided either with one or the other of the rival families, as circumstances dictated.

I have already stated that Rana Bahadur was succeeded by his illegitimate son, Maha Rajah Girivan Juddha Bikram Sah, a mere boy, and consequently, in the administration of affairs, completely guided by his minister Bheem Sing, the Sirdar of whom mention is made in the preceding paragraph, who, on His Highness' demise (by small-pox) which occurred towards the end of 1816, continued to direct the reins of Government, as Premier to his successor, Maha Rajah, Raj Rajindra Bikram Sah, an infant of only two years of age at the time of his father's decease. Upon the Rajah's attaining the age of maturity, the system of intrigue again commenced, but, notwithstanding the numerous attempts on the part of the Pandee faction to undermine his influence, this powerful and able minister retained the management of affairs until 1837, when the machinations of his enemies at last prevailed, and at the instigation of the elder Rani, who had become his bitter and implacable enemy, he was deprived of his appointment and flung into prison. Owing however to the influence of the younger Queen, a partisan of the Thapa family, he was soon after liberated, and for nearly two years the King temporized between the contending parties and abstained from nominating a minister. In the early part of 1839,* the struggles of faction attained their height, and resulted in the appointment of Ram Sing Pandee to the office of Premier; on the strength of a charge of being accessary to the murder of one of the Rajah's children, to whom it was supposed that poison had been administered, Bheem Sing was again placed in confinement. Whilst in prison, intelligence was conveyed to the ill-fated chief that the sanctity

* In the course of this year arrangements were completed with the Durbar for facilitating the adjustment of suits prosecuted by British subjects in the Nepalese Courts.

of his zenanah had been violated, and its inmates delivered up, to gratify the brutal lusts of the soldiery; excited almost to frenzy, and determined not to survive the dishonor which he imagined had befallen him, he, as his opponents calculated, committed suicide; on the 29th July, he was found in his cell, with his throat cut almost from ear to ear; his body by orders of the Rajah was carried away to the banks of the Bag Mati river, and denied all funeral rites. I have often heard it asserted, that one word from the British representative would have averted this catastrophe, but, unfortunately, when an attempt was made by some members of the court to ascertain his sentiments, he declined expressing any opinion, and from that moment the degraded minister was doomed. The Pandees having now succeeded to office, one of their first acts was to confiscate the late minister's property, and remove from his appointment almost every member of his family, of sufficient power and influence, to render him, formidable as a rival; not contented, however, with confining their attention to the internal management of their country, they would fain interfere with its foreign policy, which, with the exception of an intrigue with Scindiah in 1817, which had been detected, and the intercepted correspondence made over by the Resident to the Rajah in full Durbar, had hitherto, subsequent to the contraction of peace, if not favorable, at least, I believe, never been openly hostile to the British Alliance. No sooner, therefore, had they assumed the direction of affairs, than they originated a series of intrigues against the Indian Government at almost every Native Court throughout the country. Owing, however, to the vigilance of our Representative, aided by the exertions of the magisterial officers on the frontier, many of their letters were seized and irrefragable proof of their treacherous machinations thus discovered. This being adduced by the Resident, the Rajah was called upon, as the only way to prevent a rupture between the States, to change his advisers, and a British force of 3 troops of Cavalry, 4 regiments of Infantry, and some guns, moved to the frontier to support the demand. Not being in a position to oppose our wishes, the cogency of our reasoning was admitted, and the ministry removed, moreover, posts, which in violation of our territory had been established in the direction of Ramnuggur, for the collection of revenue from lands beyond the boundary, were withdrawn. For the next 2 or 3 years the King dispensed with assistance, and took the administration of affairs into his own hands, occasionally delegating his authority to the Heir Apparent, a boy of only 11 or 12 years of age, naturally of a most violent temper, which had been increased by habitual indulgence in acts of cruelty. On one occasion he was so far carried away by his passion, as to be induced to threaten the life of the Resident; when he was calmly informed, that thousands of our fellow countrymen would be prepared to avenge his death. The answer had its effect, and I imagine, all due amends were made for the insult offered, which, after due warning as to future behaviour, was most likely passed over as an ebullition of petulance on the part of a child. Things appear to have been conducted in a most unsatisfactory manner until the 26th December 1843, when the vacant post of Premier was again filled, by the installation of General Mahtabar Sing, a nephew of the late Bheem Sing Thapa.

This Chief bore the reputation of being an able and gallant soldier. He was also not unknown as a diplomatist, having been employed in the cold season of 1836-37, on an embassy to Calcutta. On his return to Kathmandhoo he shared the fate of his uncle, was degraded from office and imprisoned; he was however subsequently released and deputed on a mission to Runjeet

Sing. As the object of his visit was supposed hostile to the British interests, at the requisition of Captain Wade,—Political Agent at Loodianah, he was surrendered to our authorities, and for many years resided, to a certain extent, under surveillance, and in receipt of a pension of 1,000 rupees per mensem, within our territories. In April 1843, however, his political opponents at Kathmandhoo, having been deprived of their authority, he again made his appearance at court and was taken into favor, and eventually, as above stated, appointed minister. One of his first steps, after his accession to office, was to take measures for the removal of all rivals, the usual method adopted by Orientals to prevent opposition. The late Pandee ministers were immediately arrested and arraigned, for high misdemeanour, before a Council of Chiefs, who, under the Rajah's instructions, found them guilty of the charges preferred against them, and they were sentenced to be beheaded, which sentence was duly carried into effect, and in a few hours the headless trunks of 9 Sirdars lay on the banks of the Bag Mati river.

For some time he continued to direct affairs with tolerable success; but in November 1844, having proceeded with the Rajah and a large body of troops into the Terai, ostensibly on a shooting excursion, he took the opportunity, on a charge of treason, of executing no less than 16 sepoys, at a place called Duapua Basa. This act of heedless severity alienated the affection of the army, which he had hitherto enjoyed, and he soon after embroiled himself with his own relatives, under the following circumstances:—

Certain indiscretions on the part of the Rani, who, by the bye, was the daughter of a zemindar in the Gorukhpore district, having given rise to reports injurious to her reputation, a Sirdar of the Thapa family, by all accounts a careless, harum scarum sort of person, publicly stated that as the Rajah had been dishonored by the conduct of his wife, he was unfit to reign and ought accordingly to be deposed. This impolitic remark reached the Palace, and the Rani used every means at her command, to compass the death of the thoughtless speaker. At last her persuasions prevailed upon Mahtabar Sing, who had been raised to the dignity of Premier, chiefly through her partisanship, to sanction his execution, as a traitor, and he was publicly beheaded. From that moment it was evident that the Rani's influence was paramount at the Durbar, and Mahtabar Sing never recovered the confidence of his party, each of whom felt, that his life thenceforward might at any moment be sacrificed to gratify the caprice of a woman.

He was, moreover, soon after instigated by his patroness and the Rajah, to destroy some of the Sirdars of the Chountra family, who had rendered themselves obnoxious, by attempting to impose some restraint upon the royal prerogative, and refusing, in this instance, to become subservient to their wishes, or perhaps wanting the power to carry them into effect, he not only lost his former influence, but all parties, forgetting their old feuds, made common cause in conspiring against him, and 'ere long his destruction was resolved on. On the night of the 17th May 1845, about 11 o'clock, he was summoned to the Palace. The order was too peremptory to admit of his declining to attend. No sooner had he reached the apartment in which the Rajah and Rani were sitting, and approached to pay his respects, than a shot was fired by General Jung Bahadur from behind a screen at one end of the room. The unfortunate Sirdar rushed forward as if to implore mercy, but having received a mortal wound, only proceeded a few paces 'ere he fell, and was almost instantaneously dispatched by repeated blows of the Kukri, (Nepal knife) inflicted by persons in attendance on the Monarch. The murder occurred in the upper rooms of the Palace, and his body was ordered to be tied up in a blanket and thrown out of the window to the court below, where a party was in waiting to receive it, thence the corpse was dragged by ropes to the Temple of Pasupati Nath, and placed on a funeral pile previously prepared, and in half an hour, save the clouts of blood by which the road leading to the temple was plentifully besprinkled, not a vestige remained of the once all-powerful minister, and all traces of the bloody transaction had disappeared: but its remembrance cannot be banished from the mind of the principal actor in the tragedy, who has since paid the penalty of his ingratitude to his benefactor, for he was Matahbar Sing's favorite nephew, by finding that happiness is not necessarily attendant upon power, and himself experiencing the bitterness of discovering, in the recent conspiracy, those who ought to have been bound to him by every tie of affection and gratitude, arrayed in the ranks of his enemies.

With the exception of the time passed in his visit to Europe, for years he has never spent an hour free from care and anxiety; no guarantee can be said to exist for his safety even for a single moment; almost night and day he is surrounded by guards with loaded rifles, for he is well aware there are several, could they obtain the opportunity, who are quite prepared to follow the example he has set them.

I have often endeavoured to divine the motives by which General Jung Bahadur was actuated in thus accomplishing his Uncle's destruction, and feel convinced, that unscrupulous perhaps as he may be, with regard to removing any impediment to his own rise, this alone, would never have prompted him to commit so treacherous an act, and that a desire to revenge his cousin's execution, and fear of his own life, which had already been twice attempted, and which he no longer thought Mahtabar Sing would protect, were the principal causes which induced him to take a part in the conspiracy.

After the assassination of Mahtabar Sing, the different factions seem to have coalesced, and a ministry been formed accordingly. Guggun Sing, the supposed paramour of the Rani, being nominated Premier, and the second post occupied by Jung Bahadur, who was raised from the rank of Kazi, to that of General, with three regiments and the command of the army. Their colleagues in the administration were, Futteh Jung Chountra and General Abhiman Sing Rana. For upwards of a year, although occasional bickerings may have occurred, no open explosion took place between these parties; during this period, however, as respects the head of the Government, the arrangement appears to have been of rather a complicated nature; at one time the Rajah, another, the Heir Apparent, and at a third, the Rani, being considered invested with Sovereign authority, and sometimes all three assisting to guide the state chariot, but the latter was eventually appointed Regent with full powers.

On the 14th September 1846, General Guggun Sing was shot whilst sitting in his own room. Although there are persons to whom suspicion attached, and the assassin was afterwards discovered, it has never been clearly proved who was the instigator of this crime. Intelligence of the murder was immediately dispatched to the Rani, who at once proceeded to the deceased's house, and subsequently to the Kot. On reaching the latter place, she sent for General Abhiman Sing, and desired him to assemble the troops and civil authorities; meanwhile General Jung Bahadur and his brothers, with his three regiments, arrived, and the General called upon the Rani, as the acknowledged Ruler of the State, to institute a strict enquiry relative to the assassination of his colleague, stating, that in the event of its being permitted to pass unrevenged, his own life would be endangered. Whilst he was still speaking, the Maha Rajah, attended by General Abhiman Sing and many Civil and Military functionaries, for the most part unarmed, made his appearance. Bum Bahadur was then instructed by the Rani to proceed to the residence of Futteh Jung Sah Chountra, and summon that Sirdar to attend; by her orders also a Chief called Bir Kishan Pandee was put in irons, under charge of being implicated in, if not the principal instigator of, the murder; the grounds for this accusation do not appear to have transpired. Upon being questioned as to his guilt, it was strenuously denied by the accused, but little attention was paid to his asseverations of innocence, and General Abhiman Sing was directed to put him to death; as, however, the Rajah, who was in an adjoining apartment, declined sanctioning the execution, he refused to obey the Rani's mandate, and left the room. Shortly after the Rajah went out, accompanied by General Budrina Sing, and rode to Futteh Jung's house, where he had an interview with the Chountra, and ordered him to proceed to the Kot, which he accordingly did, taking with him his son, Bikram Sah, and his two brothers Bir Bahadur Sah and Runshere Sah, also Bum Bahadur, who, as already mentioned, had been dispatched in the first instance to command his attendance. On his reaching the Kot, he was met by General Jung Bahadur, who mentioned all that had occurred, and concluded by saying, that it was proper both Bir Kishan Pandee and Abhiman Sing should be put to death, and, in fact, as the Rani, having been invested with full powers, must be deemed the head of the Government, if the measure only obtained her sanction, he would himself be ready to carry it into effect, in which case Futteh Jung would assume the post of Prime Minister, whilst he would be content to retain his office of Commander-in-Chief. He at the same time pointed out, that their own safety mainly depended upon the removal of the two Sirdars, as they were notoriously inimical to them both, and would never rest satisfied until they had compassed their destruction. All his arguments were however of no avail, the Chountra could not be induced to approve of the suggestion, and put an end to the discussion by stating, that to inflict punishment before guilt was clearly established would be most unjust. The parties then separated, Futteh Jung proceeding to the apartment where Abhiman Sing was sitting, and Jung Bahadur rejoining the Rani. It was then, that the latter, finding that he could not overcome the scruples of his colleague, determined temporarily to deprive him of freedom, in order that he might be at liberty to prosecute the design which he deemed absolutely essential for their common weal. Soon after his reaching the upper story, Jung

Bahadur observed Abhiman Sing order the Officers of his corps to be on the *qui vive*, and the men were directed to load. He communicated this circumstance to the Rani, who immediately descended to the room where the Chiefs were assembled, and urged them to name the assassin of Guggun Sing. On Futteh Jung's replying that all necessary enquiry should be made, and, if possible, the merited penalty of his guilt duly inflicted on the criminal, she became highly excited, and endeavoured to use a sword she held in her hand against Bir Kishan Pandee; on being prevented, she again mounted the staircase, followed by Futteh Jung, Abhiman Sing and Kazi Dul Bhunjun Pandee. This was the opportunity seized by Jung Bahadur, to attempt to place the former under restraint. Karak Bikram Sah, seeing the attack made upon his father, and imagining that his life was at stake, determined either to save him or to avenge his death, and snatching a kukri, the only weapon he could obtain, from a Gorkha, rushed forward in a most gallant manner, and before he could be restrained, inflicted wounds on Bum Bahadur, Krishn Bahadur and a soldier, upon which he was cut down by a blow from the sword of Colonel Dhere Shumshere Bahadur. Perceiving the death of his son, the Chountra, invoking vengeance on his murderers, drew his sword, and dispersing those who surrounded him, with a bound, reached Bum Bahadur's side. The wound, which the latter had received in the right hand, prevented his defending himself, and the enraged father, raising his arm, prepared to deliver his blow with his utmost force; ere, however, it could descend, the report of a rifle rung through the hall, and when the smoke cleared away, the old Chief lay side by side with his gallant son, whose fall he had hoped to revenge. Jung Bahadur, for his was the hand that sped the deadly bullet, now saw that it was too late to retract; a moment's indecision might prove fatal alike to his power and his life. His plans were soon formed: he summoned to his side the faithful attendants, armed with double barrelled rifles, who even then hardly ever left him, and on whose fidelity he knew he could rely. They handed him their weapons duly loaded, and ere many seconds had elapsed, fourteen times successively, the sharp sound of the rifle was heard in that crowded and awestricken assembly, and fourteen Sirdars, including Abhiman Sing and Kazi Dul Bhunjun Pandee, dropped mortally wounded; the former made a last effort to join his troops in the court-yard, but before he reached the door, his body was almost cut in two by a blow from General Krishn Bahadur. Fear then took possession of the Chiefs, they turned and fled, and an indiscriminate massacre ensued. The panic even extended to the soldiery outside, and hearing the long continued peal of musketry within the building, the echoes of which reverberated in all directions, they also, with the exception of a few grenadiers of the Kali Buksh, General Jung Bahadur's own corps, all sought safety in flight. One hundred and fifty Sirdars perished on that eventful night. The slaughter was no sooner over, than the Maha Rani conferred upon Jung Bahadur the grant of the Wizarat, and accepted the usual nuzzur. This ceremony having been concluded, the new Premier at once proceeded to collect some of the troops on whom he could depend, and place them in charge of the Arsenal, Treasury, Palace, and other places of importance; these being secured, he conducted the Rani to the Hanuman Dhoka Palace, the residence of the Rajah, and then demanded an audience with the Monarch, in order that he might offer to him also the prescribed present. On being ushered into the presence of the King and Heir Apparent, the former expressed displeasure at the massacre which had taken place, and on the Jung's replying that it was in accordance with the Rani's instructions, went to her apartments to demand an explanation. Instead, however, of affording it, she advised him to place the eldest of her sons on the gaddi, (throne) which she asserted was the only means of averting further calamities. The Rajah then returned and confirmed Jung Bahadur's appointment as Prime Minister and Commander-in-Chief. It was now day-light, and a parade was ordered of all the regiments at the Capital; when the troops were assembled, Jung Bahadur, who had taken the precaution of having those faithful to his cause drawn up apart, the infantry with loaded muskets and the artillery with lighted portfires, made his appearance on the ground, and after a long and spirited harangue, in which he told the soldiers that although they had lost their former Commanders (whose bodies had been placed in a ghastly heap before them) they would find in him a sincere and stedfast friend, called upon them to obey his orders, in virtue of the authority over them vested in him by the Monarch. Without leaders, and many of them without arms, opposition would have been almost hopeless; and moreover the hearts of many were gained by the numerous promotions, consequent on the casualties amongst the Officers, which were at once promulgated. The different corps therefore returned to their cantonments without a murmur, and from that hour the army has remained devoted to the Thapa faction.

Meanwhile the Rajah, accompanied by Sirdars Bhawani Sing and Khurbeer Khuttri, the latter an adherent of Jung Bahadur, left the Palace, and started towards Patan, apparently with the intention of proceeding to Benares. Finding herself unfettered, the Rani issued orders to Jung Bahadur and Bir Dhaj Bashneat, to confiscate the property of the murdered Officers, and expel their families from Nepal, and at the same time to place the two elder Princes under surveillance.

It having been reported by Khurbeer Khuttri that the Rajah had held a private conference with Bhawani Sing on the Tundee Khel Parade ground, a party was dispatched to take the Sirdar's life. They effected their purpose on the road to Patan, in the presence of the King, who continued his route, without offering to interfere. In the evening, one of Jung Bahadur's brothers was sent in search of the fugitive Monarch, and overtaking him at Patan, persuaded him to return to Kathmandhoo. At the expiration of about eight days, order was in some measure restored, and the troops, large bodies of whom had hitherto been stationed within the city, and at the different public buildings, returned to their lines; the two Princes were not, however, released from confinement, and the Rani, in order to secure the throne for one of her own sons, used every persuasion in her power to induce Jung Bahadur to put them to death. He, however, was deaf to her entreaties, at last she was informed by Bir Dhaj Bashneat that he was convinced the Jung would never accede to her wishes, and therefore it was advisable that he also should be destroyed. As Bir Dhaj promised to aid her in the accomplishment of her design, he obtained a grant of the Wizarat. Jung Bahadur became cognizant of this transaction, through Beja Rai Pundit, who was privy to it; he was consequently on the alert, and prepared to take the first opportunity of crushing the conspirators.

On the morning of the 31st October, General Wuzeer Sing, eldest son of the late Guggun Sing, who was a party to the intended murder, secretly marched a regiment with loaded muskets to the Kot; a message was then dispatched by Bir Dhaj from the Rani, desiring Jung Bahadur's attendance; being, however, aware of the scheme to assassinate him, he had previously assembled all his friends and relatives, well armed, and in their company proceeded towards the Durbar. En route they met Bir Dhaj, who had hardly faltered out his message, for he perceived by the looks of those around him that his treachery had been discovered, ere he was killed by a blow from the sword of Captain Rana Mer Adhikari, one of the Jung's followers. The party then went to the Palace at Bussantpur, where the Rajah and his eldest son were staying, and Jung Bahadur, having been granted an interview, requested either to be dismissed from office, or to be furnished with full authority to order the execution of all enemies to the Heir Apparent. The power he demanded was delegated, and he immediately directed the troops to be placed under arms, when, with the exception of Wuzeer Sing, who had fled, all the adherents of Bir Dhaj were seized and decapitated. In the evening Jung Bahadur waited on the Rani, and on the part of the eldest Prince, stated, that as she had conspired against his life, her residence at

Kathmandhoo could no longer be sanctioned. Finding all her plans frustrated, and perceiving the inutility of attempting to make any impression upon the heart of the minister, which had now become steeled against all her charms, the lady determined to proceed on a pilgrimage to Benares. Every arrangement was made to facilitate her departure and conduce to her comfort in exile, and having been furnished with a large quantity of jewellery, &c., from the Government Tosha Khana; on the 23rd November, with her two sons, and accompanied by the Rajah, over whom she still retained a large portion of her influence, she quitted Kathmandhoo, and bent her steps towards the Holy City, where she still continues to reside.

For some time it was supposed that the Monarch only contemplated a few days temporary absence, but when months elapsed and he evinced no intention of returning to his Kingdom, after due deliberation, it was resolved that his voluntary exile could only be construed into an act of abdication, and his crown must devolve upon the Heir Apparent, who had hitherto carried on the Government as Regent: on the 12th May 1847, he was consequently installed as Sovereign. Upon intelligence of this proceeding reaching Benares, the Ex-King, instigated most likely by his Rani, whose ambition was evidently too great to admit of her tamely allowing her husband to forfeit his dignity without a struggle, determined to make an effort to regain his throne, and accordingly set out for the frontier. His movements were, however, most closely watched, and arrangements made for intercepting his advance towards the Capital, where it is possible he might have been still able to form a powerful party. Whilst within the British possessions, he was escorted by a guard of Irregular Cavalry, which returned to their cantonments on his crossing the border on the 28th July. As soon as the news of the departure of this detachment reached Kathmandhoo, orders were issued for the march of several corps in the direction of the King's encampment; in one day they descended the hills, and towards evening took up positions in its immediate neighbourhood. Little anticipating such prompt and decisive measures, the Rajah's adherents were calmly reposing in fancied security, when they were suddenly recalled to the recollection of their having passed the fatal boundary, by finding themselves completely surrounded by their enemies. Although thus taken by surprise, they bravely defended themselves, and endeavoured to beat off their assailants, but being perfectly devoid of organization, their ill-directed efforts proved of no avail. A scene of the greatest confusion ensued; little loss was experienced by the troops, and in fact it soon became a mere massacre. Four or five hundred were killed and wounded, the rest escaped to our territories, and the Monarch, completely deserted, was taken prisoner and conducted to Kathmandhoo, where he still remains, under strict surveillance, and deprived of all political power. He is certainly produced at the Durbar on important occasions, such for instance as the presentation of Her Majesty's letter, but apparently takes little interest in what is going forward, casting, however, furtive glances in every direction, as if to fathom, from the looks of those around him, the cause of his temporary elevation, and fearing lest it is only preparatory to some act of treachery, by which all dread of his re-accession to Sovereign rank may be finally dissipated, and himself removed from all further concern with sublunary affairs.

The complete overthrow of both the Chountras and Pandees having been accomplished, and the Rajah reduced to a mere cipher, the whole power of the Government seems to have become concentrated in the person of Jung Bahadur, who has shown

2 x

himself well worthy of the trust which has thus devolved upon him, having diligently exerted himself to root out abuses, and effect salutary reforms in all departments, and, if his life be spared, he may yet be the means of introducing great improvements throughout the country. In Nepal, however, fortune has for years truly proved herself a fickle jade, and it yet remains to be seen whether his fate will differ from that of his predecessors. In carrying out his views he derived the utmost assistance from the late Rani, a talented and amiable woman, whose influence over her husband was always exerted in Jung Bahadur's favor, and he was thus enabled to guide the weak and imbecile Monarch, without incurring the necessity of ever openly opposing his authority. It is said that on one occasion this influence was successfully exerted to prevent a rupture with the British, advocated by several of the Minister's enemies, with a view to effect his ruin, as had he objected, he would have been branded as a coward, and lost his popularity with the army; whilst, on the contrary, if war had been declared, and the Nepalese forces, as expected, routed, he would have been stigmatized as a traitor, and in all probability fallen a victim to some popular ebullition. Be this as it may, it is certain that he experienced from the Rani the greatest kindness, and bitterly deplored her loss.

The object of the late Mission to England was not only to offer homage to the Sovereign of that Nation, whose Statesmen and Warriors, to use the Ambassador's own expression, had rendered the name of Great Britain glorious throughout the East, nor was it merely for the purpose of making himself acquainted with the actual extent of our power and the true cause of our greatness, although these reasons doubtless had their due weight in prompting a step so totally repugnant to all the prejudices of Hinduism, and which may perhaps prove the first blow towards breaking the apparently almost insurmountable barrier, which now prevents the Natives of India from seeking, in travel through foreign countries, liberal sentiments and enlightened opinions, but although never publicly acknowledged, there was another great inducement, viz. the hope that in firmly uniting the bonds of friendship between the States, he would also materially strengthen his own position, from the feeling, which, notwithstanding the policy of non-interference professed by the Indian Government, would pervade all classes in Nepal, that the minister who had been honored by an audience with the Queen of England, would never want assistance in the hour of need.

This cursory glance at the history of Nepal would certainly be incomplete, were I not to offer some slight account of the actor who for the last few years has played so important a part upon the stage. I shall therefore conclude with a brief sketch of his eventful life.

General Jung Bahadur is descended from a good family, both his paternal and maternal grandfathers having held high rank in Ummur Sing's army, and been engaged at the siege of Kot Khangra, where one was killed and the other mortally wounded. His father, who held the office of Kazi, had eight sons, of whom he is the second. When a lad of about 14 years of age he was attached as Subahdar to a regiment under his father's command, and stationed on the north-western frontier. Tired of the common routine of military life, he quitted his corps without permission, and with a single attendant crossed the Kali Nuddee and entered the Company's territories. As long as his resources lasted, he employed his time in traversing the whole of the provinces of Rohilkund, and visiting our Military Stations in that direction; on reaching Hurdwar, however, he found that not only had he completely exhausted his stock of cash, but also disposed of every article of value he possessed. He accordingly contemplated offering his sword to Runjeet Sing, in whose service he had relatives; but meeting with some of his father's friends, he was persuaded to return to his duty, and, his youth being taken into consideration in extenuation of the fault which he had committed in deserting his post, he was re-admitted to his former rank. Soon after, the fall of Bheem Sing Thapa having destroyed his hopes of advancement, he left the army, and for sometime wandered throughout Nepal, making himself perfectly acquainted with the topography of the country, and also with the dialects, manners and customs of the different tribes composing its inhabitants. On his return to Kathmandhoo, an elephant, having become *must*, in this infuriated state became perfectly ungovernable, and, killing its mahout, entered the crowded city, creating havoc and consternation in every direction; no one dared approach to arrest its wild career, but Jung

Bahadur, having watched his opportunity, flung himself from the top of a house upon the animal's neck, blindfolded it with a cloth, and eventually succeeded in securing it to a tree. The fame of this daring exploit having reached the Durbar, he was sent for, and offered a dress of honor and a sum of money, which, however, he refused, but demanded promotion, and accordingly received a Lieutenant's commission. His rise may be calculated from the date of the performance of this feat, for although hostile to the party in power, they were glad to avail themselves of his services, and in 1839, he was raised to the rank of Captain, and employed on a secret mission to Benares, for the purpose of seizing and carrying off to Nepal, Runodutt Sah Chountra, a brother of the present Ex-Rajah, who was then residing at that City. His endeavours, however, proved unavailing, and his intentions having been discovered by the British authorities, he was at first incarcerated, and afterwards escorted by the Police to the Nepal frontier, where he was released. After this unsuccessful expedition, he seems to have chiefly distinguished himself by his advocacy of measures of reform in the administration of public affairs, thereby rendering himself obnoxious to the ruling Chiefs, who took every opportunity of prejudicing the Rajah and Heir Apparent against him, and trying to take his life. On one occasion, whilst in the act of crossing on horseback a mountain stream, by a bridge, composed merely of the trunks of two trees, he received the commands of the King to return: had he refused compliance with the order, he would have been charged with disloyalty, whilst it was supposed that the attempt to obey, would ensure his destruction, for a false step would have precipitated him down an abyss of several hundred feet, and dashed him to atoms. His pony was fortunately extremely surefooted, and with admirable presence of mind, he succeeded in making the animal perform a pirouette, and reached the bank in safety. On another day, the bridge having, on some pretext or other, been removed before he had passed, he was summoned to the King's presence on the opposite side of a similar stream. He attempted the leap, but his horse, being unable to cover the required distance, he was plunged into the torrent, and carried down by its force nearly a mile ere he was able to effect a landing, and at last, failing to compass his death by indirect means, his enemies prevailed upon the Prince to issue orders for his execution; in accordance with which he was flung into a deep well, but being an expert swimmer, managed to support himself for hours in the water, and at night, when his friends came with the intention of taking out the body, he was discovered alive, but perfectly exhausted, with his nails almost torn off from clinging to the brick work. His path therefore has not been without its thorns and he has not gained his present position without undergoing the ordeal to which all men of rank in Oriental Courts are necessarily exposed.

As a Minister, Jung Bahadur's life has been almost without reproach, and he has laboured incessantly for the welfare of the country, over whose destinies it may be said, he at present presides. When he first obtained his office, he was extremely illiterate, and, owing to wilfulness when a child, could neither read nor write. Finding that without these acquirements he was liable to be misled by those around him, and consequently to act unjustly, he devoted all his leisure hours to study, and at the expiration of a year had obtained such proficiency as to be able to carry on a correspondence with perfect facility, and all orders of importance are written with his own hand. Towards the Chiefs, although not unkind, he is certainly dictatorial in manner, and has thus made enemies amongst them, but he is much loved both by the Troops and Peasantry, and I believe no act of cruelty or injustice can be urged against him from the date of his accession to power, whilst hundreds of his political opponents and their adherents, who had been banished from the country, have been permitted to return, on the *sole proviso*, that they shall remain on their estates, and not make their appearance at the capital.

No excuse can certainly be offered in palliation of his guilt in taking so prominent a part in the murder of his Uncle Mahtabar Sing, through whose influence he had been raised to the rank of Chief Kazi, and from whom, almost to within a short time of his death, he had experienced the utmost kindness; but in judging of the conduct of a Native of the East, is it just on our part to adopt the Christian standard of morality, or rather ought we not to remember that he has been debarred the pure light of the gospel to guide and restrain him, amidst the numerous temptations to which he is exposed throughout his worldly career, and consequently that our condemnation should be mingled with pity? The act which may be considered the second blot in his life, the massacre at the Kot, he has always asserted, and I believe with truth, to have been perfectly unpremeditated, and that, although under the impression that Abhiman Sing and Bir Kishan Pandee were the instigators of Guggun Sing's assassination, he had determined at all hazards to secure their execution, he never for a moment contemplated treachery towards his colleague Futteh Jung, and even at the last instant, when his brother's life hung as it were upon a thread, he hesitated ere he fired the fatal shot.

Jung Bahadur is brave, active, and daring, at the same time not devoid of caution, combined with a great degree of innate shrewdness, and possessing considerable talent, together with determination and self-possession, all qualities conducing to form an admirable Military Commander. He is extremely observant, and his remarks on men and manners, betray a knowledge of the world denoting the deep study of human nature, and little to be expected from one who had spent his days in such a remote region. Although not only a just, but by all accounts a decidedly mild ruler, and naturally far from being cruel or prone to deeds of violence, self-interest is ever with him the predominant passion. The sacrifice of human life would have but little weight in preventing the prosecution of any design on which he might be bent, and the expediency of the measure would fully satisfy all scruples which he might have on that head. To his friends he is often extremely generous, but his acts of generosity are generally committed on the impulse of the moment, and can hardly be said to spring from the dictates of a truly liberal heart.

Although, like all Orientals, a perfect master of the art of dissimulation, and embued with a feeling of suspicion of those around him, plainly discernible in all his acts and words, when thoroughly convinced that he is treated with perfect candour, he at once banishes all reserve, and converses unrestrainedly on topics either connected with his own life or relative to his country, notwithstanding that in so doing, he may make acknowledgments prejudicial to his interests. He has an active, and enquiring mind, and is fully impressed with the great advantages which might accrue to Nepal from the introduction of the arts and sciences of Western civilization, whilst however, a still lurking doubt as to the sincerity of our professions of friendship, which his trip to Europe has not completely removed, may for many years preclude his seeking our aid in carrying into execution the projects he now entertains towards improving the country and ameliorating the condition of the people, and which he is sensible cannot be accomplished without our cordial co-operation and assistance. Taking into consideration the fact of his having been reared at a dissolute and corrupt court, amongst a nation barely removed from a state of barbarism, whilst almost from boyhood his passions have remained uncontrolled, Jung Bahadur has a fair claim to our estimation. He is far in advance of his fellow countrymen, and whilst his faults may be attributed to his race and education, his virtues are all his own.

I have now brought my labors to a close, and solicit the indulgence of my readers for having inflicted upon their patience the task of perusing so dull a volume. Thus much, however, I must say in my defence, that the work has never claimed to be considered more than its title assumes, viz. a mere Series of Rough Notes, taken in my capacity as a Political Officer, without intent to publication; arrogating in themselves no pretensions to favor, but deriving some slight interest from their presenting a sketch, imperfect as it may be, of a Country, of which, notwithstanding its contiguity to our Noble Empire in the East, we are so little acquainted, either as respects its History, Topography, the Religion, Manners, and Customs of the numerous tribes by which it is inhabited, its Government, Manufactures, or Commerce: a Country, moreover, which may now fairly advance some slight claim to our regard, as the first Hindu State, from which, casting aside their long cherished and inveterate prejudices, an Embassy has issued, to pay obeisance at the Court of our Most Gracious Queen.

APPENDIX.

Treaty between the Hon'ble the East India Company and the Raja of Nepal.

ARTICLE 1ST.—There shall be perpetual peace and friendship between the Hon'ble East India Company and the Raja of Nepal.

ARTICLE 2ND.—The Raja of Nepal renounces all claim to the lands which were the subject of discussion between the two states before the war; and acknowledges the right of the Hon'ble Company to the sovereignty of those lands.

ARTICLE 3RD.—The Raja of Nepal hereby cedes to the Hon'ble the East India Company in perpetuity, all the undermentioned territories, namely—

First,—The whole of the lowlands between the Rivers Kali and Raptee.

Secondly.—The whole of the lowlands (with the exception of Bootwul Khas) lying between the Raptee and the Gunduk.

Thirdly.—The whole of the lowlands between the Gunduk and Koosee, in which the authority of the British Government has been introduced, or is in actual course of introduction.

Fourthly.—All the lowlands between the River Mechee and the Teesta.

Fifthly—All the territories within the hills, eastward of the River Mechee, including the fort and lands of Nagree, and the pass of Nagareote, leading from Morung into the hills, together with the territory lying between that pass and Nagree. The aforesaid territory shall be evacuated by the Gorkha troops within forty days from this date.

ARTICLE 4TH.—With a view to indemnify the Chiefs and barahdars of the State of Nepal, whose interests will suffer by the alienation of the lands ceded by the foregoing Article, the British Government agrees to settle pensions, to the aggregate amount of two lacs of rupees per annum, on such Chiefs as may be selected by the Raja of Nepal, and in the proportions which the Raja may fix. As soon as the selection is made, sunuds shall be granted under the seal and signature of the Governor General for the pensions, respectively.

ARTICLE 5TH.—The Raja of Nepal renounces, for himself, his heirs, and suceessors, all claims to, or connexion with, the countries lying to the west of the River Kali; and engages never to have any concern with these countries or the inhabitants thereof.

ARTICLE 6TH.—The Raja of Nepal engages never to molest or disturb the Raja of Sikhim in the possession of his territories, but agrees, if any differences shall arise between the State of Nepal and the Raja of Sikhim, or the subjects of either, that such differences shall be referred to the arbitration of the British Government, by whose award the Raja of Nepal engages to abide.

ARTICLE 7TH.—The Raja of Nepal hereby engages never to take or retain in his service any British subject, nor the subject of any European or American state, without the consent of the British Government.

ARTICLE 8TH.—In order to secure and improve the relations of amity and peace hereby established between the two States, it is agreed that accredited Ministers from each shall reside at the Court of the other.

Treaty between the Hon'ble the East India Company and the Raja of Sikhim.

ARTICLE 1ST.—The Hon'ble East India Company cedes, transfers, and makes over, in full sovereignty, to the Sikhimputee Raja, his heirs, or successors, all the hilly or mountainous country situated to the eastward of the Mechee River, and to the westward of the Teesta River, formerly possessed and occupied by the Raja of Nepal ceded to the Hon'ble East India Company by the treaty of peace signed at Segowlee.

ARTICLE 2ND.—The Sikhimputee Raja engages, for himself and successors, to abstain from any acts of aggression or hostility against the Gorkhas, or any other state.

ARTICLE 3RD.—That he will refer to the arbitration of the British Government any disputes or questions that may arise between his subjects, and those of Nepal, or any other neighbouring State, and abide by the decision of the British Government.

ARTICLE 4TH.—He engages for himself and successors to join the British troops with the whole of his Military Force, when employed within the hills, and in general to afford the British troops every aid and facility in his power.

ARTICLE 5TH.—That he will not permit any British subjects nor the subject of any European or American State, to reside within his dominions without the permission of the English Government.

ARTICLE 6TH—That he will immediately seize and deliver up any dacoits, or notorious offenders, that may take refuge within his territories.

ARTICLE 7TH.—That he will not afford protection to any defaulters of revenue, or other delinquents, when demanded by the British Government through their accredited agents.

ARTICLE 8TH.—That he will afford protection to merchants and traders from the Company's provinces; and he engages that no duties shall be levied on the transit of merchandize beyond the established custom at the several golahs and marts.

ARTICLE 9TH.—The Hon'ble East India Company guarantees to the Sikhimputee Raja and his successors, the full and peaceable possession of the tract of hilly country specified in the first Article of the present agreement.

Routes into Nepal.

I.

Semul Basa to Bicheeah Khor,	...	10	miles.
„ to Hetoundah,	...	14	„
„ to Bheem Phedee,	...	18	„
„ to Seesa Gurhee,	...	3	„
„ to Tambu Khani,	...	6	„
„ to Makhoo	...	1	„
To Kathmandhoo *via* Chitlong,	...	18	„
„ Pher Phing,	...	22	„

This road has been described in the 1st Chapter. It is said that tho best route into the valley of Kathmandhoo turns to the West at Bicheeah Khor, continuing its course for about 8 miles, when it takes a northerly direction, it is represented as being generally about 30 feet in breadth, level and winding between the bases of steep hills. Horses, carriages and elephants may pass along it, as there are no large rivers nor mountains to be crossed.

II.

Bootwul to Nyakot,	...	...	...	3	coss.
„ to Masseean,	...	...	...	5	„
„ to Palpa,	...	...	...	6	„
„ to 1st halting place,			...	4	„
„ to 2nd ditto,	...	...	...	5	„
„ to Rampore,	...	...	...	8	„

The road to Palpa is mentioned as being about 5 feet in breadth, and leading in a zigzag direction over two very steep and long ascents, besides others of inferior height, it is throughout passable by hill ponies and small elephants, accustomed to the country. About 8 coss from Bootwul it crosses the Tinavee River, the channel about 50 yards wide, bed rocky, banks not very steep, water knee-deep. From Palpa the route takes an easterly direction, and runs principally through Sal Forests. It passes over 2 steep mountains and several small hills. Rampore is situated on a large plain near the bank of the great Gunduk, which is crossed by a ferry, the boat being dragged by ropes from either bank. The river at this point is upwards of 100 yards wide, and flowing with great rapidity over the rocks which form its bed.

III.

1st. Stage. From Chutra on the East Bank of the Koosi to Mayna and Lasunuja, crossing the Koosi and Sankoosi.

2nd Stage to Kula.
3rd „ Khatang.
4th „ Kamteb.
5th „ Halisi, at the junction of the Dudh Koosi.
6th „ Teleya.
7th „ Baugman, on the west side of the Lekho.
8th „ Mautaligaut, west side of the Tamba Koosi.
9th „ Pachigaut, on the Sankoosi.
10th „ Dumja, on the Rusi.
11th „ Dapcha, on the north side of the Rusi.
12th „ Banipa, at the head of the Rusi.
13th „ Bhatgaon.

At all the Stages above mentioned, it is said there are villages, and by the way there is much cultivation. The valley of the Sankoosi is stated to be from one to two miles in width, and for the greater part of the distance the traveller may ride on horseback.

IV.

From Sesoutwa to	Giria Pokhun,	...	2 coss.
	Mehooleea,	...	1 „
	Jugulpoor,	...	2 „
	Hureeon Betheon,	...	2½ „
	Bhumthan Choree,	...	4 „
	Ruttunpoor,	...	3 „
	Hurreehurpoor,	...	2½ „

This route is the one alluded to at page 30.

From Kathmandhoo to Diggurcha, or Teeshoo Loomboo by Kooti Goojeperri near Pusputnath, or Deopatun.

From Kathmandhoo	to Sankoo E. N. E.	...	9 miles.
„	to Deopoor, E. B. N.	...	14 „
„	to Seepa, E. B. N.	...	13 „
„	to Jhauri, E. B. N.	...	2 „
„	to Chawtra, E. N. E. or N. E. B. N.	...	14 „
„	to Pyhiere, E. N. E.	...	14 „
„	to Phulloo, N. N. E.	...	14 „
„	to Leistee, N. N. E.	...	8 „
„	to Doogna, N. N. E.	...	10 „
„	to Khasa, N. E.	...	19 „
„	to Chesuing, N. N. E.	...	12 „

From Chesuing	to Kooti, N. N. E.	12	miles.
„	to Soonagoombah, E. B. N. ...	11	„
„	to Mathiegoombah, N. E. ...	14	„
„	to Lungoorphedi, E.	12	„
„	to Lungkoat, E. & N. B. E. ...	22	„
„	to Tingri, E.	12	„
„	to Ghuttiapani, E.	18	„
„	to Neckagoombah, E. ...	5	„
„	to Koonagoombah, E. ...	16	„
„	to Shikargoombah, E. ...	3	„
„	to Shikar Dhoban, E. ...	8	„
„	to Dhairebaihra-Katra Kagong, E.	10	„
„	to Chhogoomba, E.	4	„
„	to Choorbaloon, E.	8	„
„	to Saitagoombah, E.	16	„
„	to Bhysiagong, N.	12	„
„	to Sankia, E.	11	„
„	to Ekelagoombah, E. & N. ...	18	„
„	to Shangookabaissa, E. B. N. or E. N. E.	14	„
„	to Loll Pahar, E.	12	„
„	to Kaghizi Goombah, E. ...	25	„
„	to Diggurcha, or Teeshoo Lombah, E.	10	„
	Total, miles, ...	279	

Meteorological Register, Kathmandhoo, 1825.

Months.	Inside the House.				Outside in the Shade.				Remarks.
	A. M. 8	A. M. 12	P. M. 4	P. M. 10	A. M. 8	A. M. 12	P. M. 4	P. M. 10	
January, ...	$50\frac{8}{31}$	$52\frac{5}{31}$	$53\frac{24}{31}$	$53\frac{18}{31}$	$37\frac{12}{31}$	$48\frac{10}{31}$	$53\frac{20}{31}$	43	Mornings foggy, days fine, occasional showers towards the end.
February, ...	$52\frac{20}{28}$	$53\frac{27}{28}$	$55\frac{23}{28}$	$54\frac{22}{28}$	$41\frac{12}{28}$	$52\frac{18}{28}$	$56\frac{9}{28}$	$46\frac{4}{28}$	Occasional fogs during the mornings, days cloudy, transient storms, accompanied by strong west wind, rain and thunder.
March, ...	$55\frac{8}{31}$	$56\frac{12}{31}$	$58\frac{16}{31}$	$56\frac{27}{31}$	$45\frac{5}{31}$	$63\frac{4}{31}$	$65\frac{10}{31}$	$51\frac{4}{31}$	Weather foggy in the mornings, during the early part of the month, days fine, with strong cool breezes from the West. Occasional showers towards the middle of the month; cloudy weather towards the latter end, with short storms of rain and thunder during the afternoons.

MONTHS.	Inside the House.				Outside in the Shade.				REMARKS.
	A. M. 8	A. M. 12	P. M. 4	P. M. 10	P. M. 8	A. M. 12	P. M. 4	A. M. 10	
April, ...	$63\frac{1}{30}$	$66\frac{2}{30}$	$67\frac{21}{30}$	$66\frac{15}{30}$	$63\frac{13}{30}$	$78\frac{28}{30}$	$78\frac{20}{30}$	$61\frac{16}{30}$	On the 10th a frost in the evening; 16th, snow fell during the night in the adjacent mountain tops. With the exception of five days, the weather throughout the month was cloudy. Towards the afternoon and at sunset violent storms from N. W. with heavy rain and thunder.
May, ...	$68\frac{18}{31}$	$70\frac{14}{31}$	$71\frac{25}{31}$	$70\frac{22}{31}$	$70\frac{30}{31}$	$83\frac{8}{31}$	$81\frac{8}{31}$	$67\frac{17}{31}$	Weather cloudy and unsettled through the month; occasional heavy showers, accompanied by thunder.
June, ...	$73\frac{5}{35}$	$74\frac{28}{30}$	$76\frac{5}{30}$	$74\frac{20}{30}$	$76\frac{5}{30}$	$85\frac{5}{30}$	$82\frac{16}{30}$	$71\frac{20}{31}$	Fine weather, with occasional showers, till towards the latter

									end of the month, weather then cloudy, with heavy rain and thunder.
July, ...	0	0	0	0	$76\frac{16}{31}$	$86\frac{8}{31}$	$82\frac{13}{31}$	$72\frac{21}{31}$	Rainy weather, with occasional sunshine.
August	0	0	0	0	$73\frac{27}{31}$	$82\frac{17}{31}$	$79\frac{5}{31}$	$71\frac{20}{31}$	Rainy weather; mornings foggy towards the latter end; on the 4th a shock of an earthquake.
September, ...	$70\frac{3}{30}$	$75\frac{10}{30}$	$76\frac{11}{30}$	75	$70\frac{23}{30}$	$77\frac{28}{30}$	$80\frac{21}{31}$	$69\frac{17}{31}$	Cloudy weather, with rain and thunder, during the first half month; foggy mornings and fine days, during the remainder.
October,... ...	$67\frac{23}{31}$	$69\frac{30}{31}$	$72\frac{17}{31}$	$69\frac{24}{31}$	$62\frac{29}{31}$	$70\frac{5}{31}$	$71\frac{18}{31}$	$62\frac{20}{31}$	Dense fogs in the mornings till 9 A. M., succeeded by very fine days, with occasional transient showers of rain.
November, ...	0	$62\frac{1}{30}$	$63\frac{24}{30}$	0	0	$59\frac{11}{30}$	$62\frac{28}{30}$	0	Dense fogs every morning; days very fine.
December, ...	0	$56\frac{13}{31}$	$58\frac{6}{31}$	0	0	$54\frac{11}{31}$	$53\frac{19}{31}$	0	Dense fogs every morning; days very fine; sharp frosts in the evenings, during the latter end of the month.

Maximum and Minimum Temperature of each month.	Max.	Min.	Max.	Min.	Max.	Min.	Max.	Min.	Max.	Min.	Max.	Min.	Max.	Min.	Max.	Min.
	A. M. 8	A. M. 8	P. M. 12	P. M. 12	P. M. 4	P. M. 4	P. M. 10	P. M. 10	A. M. 8	A. M. 8	A. M. 12	A. M. 12	P. M. 4	P. M. 4	P. M. 10	P. M. 10
January, ...	53	48	56	50	56	52½	55	52	47	28	57	44	60½	47	50	38
February, ...	55	49	56½	51	58½	54	57	52	46	32	58	47½	65¼	48	50	39
March, ...	65	48	66	51	73	53	68	52	65	32	82	49	81	54	66	40
April, ...	66	58	68	63	70	66	68	65	71	57	84	73	84	74	68	51
May, ...	73	65½	74	67	70	69	74	68	81	63	92	71	90	71	72	62
June, ...	76	70	78	72	81	73	78	72	82	67	94	70	97	72½	78	67
July, ...	...	...	...	...	...	...	...	...	84	71	94	82	86	69	78	70
August, ...	...	...	...	...	...	...	...	...	80	68½	92	73	83	72	75	68
September, ...	78	70	73	74	82	74	78	73	76¼	65	83	71	83	71	74	66
October, ...	72	62	75	63	77¼	66	76	66	71	56	76	62	78	65	69	57
November, ...	...	...	67½	58	69	60	...	...	...	...	65	55	68½	58½	...	...
December, ...	...	...	60	54	62	56	...	...	...	...	59	52	60	44	...	...

INDEX.

I.

J.

K.

L.